Praise for *Dear Denise: Letters to the Sister I Never Knew*

"Lisa bares her heart and soul about growing up with love and admiration in the light, not the shadow, of her sister Denise, whose young life was taken from her family by hate through the 1963 bombing of Birmingham's 16th Street Baptist Church. What an extraordinary expression of love and developmental bond to a sister who she never had the pleasure of meeting. She speaks truth to power, bridging the past and present and exploring her inner strength to combat racism from all members of society."

—REENA EVERS-EVERETTE, executive director of
the Medgar and Myrlie Evers Institute

"In *Dear Denise*, Lisa McNair takes the reader on a journey that at some point in our lives we all wish we could have: a conversation with a family member we never knew. In writing her letters to a sister who died in what should have been a safe place—her church—at the hands of white supremacists, Lisa in actuality has a conversation with Denise, walking the reader through the history of Birmingham and America, and her family, while continuing to seek the truths about our past and the direction for our future. It is conversations like these that will help us form that more perfect union we know as America."

—SENATOR DOUG JONES, author of *Bending Toward Justice: The
Birmingham Church Bombing that Changed the Course of Civil Rights*

"In 1997 I Directed My 1st Documentary *4 Little Girls*. It Tells The Story Of The Beautiful Young Black Girls Who Were Murdered In A Domestic Terrorist Bombing Of The 16th Street Baptist Church In Birmingham, Alabama. During And After The Production I Became Friends With The Parents Of Denise McNair. One Of The 4 Little Girls That Was Murdered. Through My Friendship With Maxine And Chris McNair, I Met Lisa McNair The Younger Sister Of Denise. This Book Is The Riveting Story Of Her Life, Her Parents, And Sister During The Volatile Era Of The Jim Crow South, And The Capital Of That BOMB-MING-HAM. Lisa Takes Us On A Stirring Trip Of Stirring Moments Of HIS/HERSTORY In These Un-United States."

—SPIKE LEE

"Lisa McNair's letters to her sister come from her heart. They are about growing up not having met Denise, who was murdered by members of the Ku Klux Klan.

Denise and three other young girls were taken in the bombing of the 16th Street Baptist Church, a sacred space, in a dynamite explosion set by the hands of local white Alabama terrorists. Lisa tells her story of searching for meaning in America, which has a history drenched in the blood of white supremacy over 400 years and continuing to this day. Lisa McNair's book is a must-read for all Americans."

—DAVID GOODMAN, the Andrew Goodman Foundation

Dear Denise

One day, while doing some deep spring-cleaning, I found your diary in a living-room closet. At first, I was thrilled at the possibility that it might help me learn more about you. But in fact it yielded little insight into your life; you were only able to make a few entries before your death, and those you did write were just a little girl's brief accounts of mundane, daily life— Christmas gifts, boys, watching *The Flintstones*. Still, I treasure this diary. Photo by Lisa McNair.

Dear Denise

↦ LETTERS TO THE SISTER I NEVER KNEW ↤

LISA McNAIR

THE UNIVERSITY OF ALABAMA PRESS

Tuscaloosa

The University of Alabama Press
Tuscaloosa, Alabama 35487-0380
uapress.ua.edu

Typeface: Garamond Premier Pro

Cover image: Denise McNair, shortly before her death, holding
her favorite doll. Photo by Chris McNair
Cover design: Lori Lynch

Note: Some pseudonyms have been used in this book to protect the privacy of nonpublic individuals.

Cataloging-in-Publication data is available from the Library of Congress.
ISBN: 978-0-8173-2135-2
E-ISBN: 978-0-8173-9416-5

—

This book is dedicated to Paula Baker Carroll, my friend and former classmate and, most importantly, the first person who really understood the struggle I was going through. When I told you how troubled and misunderstood I felt—not feeling Black enough to fit in a Black world and not white enough to fit in a white world, either—it was a big step for me, since I had not told anyone else. When I opened my heart to you, you said you were feeling and experiencing the same things. Then we both began to cry. For the first time I took a deep breath and inhaled, knowing that I was not alone on this walk. At least one person understood me—your honesty helped me live another day. I am your friend for life because of what you gave me that day. May God always be with you.

Contents

Acknowledgments

I want to give a special thanks to Reverend Doctor John Stanko, who has held my feet to the fire to get this book finished. I thank God He sent you my way. God bless you and your ministry.

Thank you, Anil Mujumdar. You were the first person I allowed to read my original manuscript. I have kept it very close to me and shared it with no one else before the publishing process began. Your opinion of my book meant more to me than I can say. The fact that you are a voracious reader and you thought what I wrote was amazing filled me with joy and confirmed my hopes for this book. You introduced me to the UA Press and they made the dream of my book come true. I owe you a debt of gratitude. Thank you for believing in my book and in me.

I want to thank April Autrey Deal. She believed in my book and looked forward to seeing it published. She continued to encourage me over the years. Sadly, she passed away just as I finished it and never got to read it. I will never forget her pushing me and believing in me.

Thank you, Todd Allen and Audra Gray, for practically harassing me on a regular basis to get this book finished. I never was offended by your pushing me. I knew that you knew that I had something very important to say with this memoir. Thanks for encouraging me and being my friend.

Thanks to Sherrill Wheeler Stewart for giving me the idea of writing my memoir in the form of letters to Denise. It was a brilliant suggestion and it made my words flow. Thanks, my friend.

And, last but not least, I want to give a very big thank you to Dan Waterman, Joanna Jacobs, and the wonderful people at the UA Press for seeing what I saw in this book and wanting to publish it for me. Dan has been amazing to work with; so patient and kind. He held my hand through this entire process, which was a bit scary at times. Joanna, your edits were amazing. You have a tremendous gift. You both made it a wonderful experience that I will always treasure.

Dear Denise

Introduction

When I think about the early part of my life, I often think of Dr. Martin Luther King Jr.'s closing remarks in his "I Have a Dream" speech to the record-setting crowd of people at the March on Washington in August 1963. Dr. King talked about how he had a dream that one day all of God's children, Black people and white people, Jews and Gentiles, Protestants and Catholics, would sing the old Negro spiritual, "Free at last, Free at last, thank God almighty, We are free at last." For me, I took that to mean that we would be free to live and love together in this country with whomever and wherever we wanted. Dr. King wanted Black people and white people not just to coexist in peace in this country but to live as friends.

Before I knew of Dr. King or of his famous speech, that dream of unity and love was always my heart's desire because my earliest memory in life was the knowledge that my older sister, Denise McNair, was one of the four little girls killed in the infamous 1963 bombing of the 16th Street Baptist Church in Birmingham, Alabama, less than three weeks after Dr. King shared his dream of a loving and just society with the world. I learned early that her death was at the hands of white men who were members of a hate-filled group of people called the Ku Klux Klan, who didn't like my people just because of the color of our skin. I knew firsthand the result that hate and divisiveness can bring. It not only could bring anger, it could bring death.

I have always been one to dream with my heart, and I think that's what Dr. King did on that day—like so many other African Americans before him. Dr. King's dream was the unspoken, heartfelt desire of many of us in America, Black as well as white. He spoke our collective dreams of freedom and equality into reality before we were really ready, as a society, to accept them. The transition from the dream to reality has been far more complicated than most people imagined.

I am living in the reality of Dr. King's dream. I am part of the first generation of African Americans who didn't grow up under the direct oppression of Jim Crow. I was born in 1964, the year in which the tragedies of 1963 produced many of the key victories over segregation and racial discrimination for African Americans. Of course, I am not pretending that racism does not exist today or that there are not countless inequities still present in the United States for African Americans and people of color, but today's world is very different than it was before I was born.

My peers and I have not been told that we cannot eat at a certain restaurant or that we have to enter the movie theater through the side entrance and sit only in the balcony. We were never restricted to drink from a particular water fountain; nor were we told we couldn't go to school with white students because of our skin color. My life has been just the opposite in many ways. My parents wanted all of the new freedoms for African Americans that followed the passage of the Civil Rights Act to be available to my baby sister and me. They enrolled us in a predominantly white private elementary school. This afforded us the opportunity to socialize with white students in a way that had not been possible for African American children of earlier generations. It also gave us the chance to expand our educational opportunities like never before. Because these and other desegregated life experiences were new, our parents had no idea how to prepare us for these transitions. For the most part we were given instructions on how to behave as respectful citizens when we entered these uncharted environments. Our parents wanted us to be dignified, but, more important, to behave in a way that would keep us from being assaulted or killed, and also to show the white race that Black people had manners and self-respect too.

This is where the conflict began for me and is my key reason for writing this book. I think of it as "being Black but growing up white." Although I was living "the dream," for me and many like me it came with its own difficulties because my life was a departure from the traditional Black experience in Alabama and in much of the south. Instead of these new experiences being celebrated or appreciated by members of my own community, I was sometimes criticized, chastised, ostracized, and even called a "white girl." I was often told I wasn't Black enough. For some in my community, I was too much like white people, who for so many centuries had been the enemy of my people. For me, I just assimilated to the environment around me. I knew of nothing different to do. The fact that I had white friends in school felt to me like I was living out Dr. King's dream, yet these same friendships did not sit well with some of my Black family and friends. This hurt me deeply because as a child I was just living my life, doing what I was told, and going along with the life that was placed before me. I was simply exploring life and had no idea that I was breaking some social norms.

This inner turmoil was difficult for me to overcome for many years. Feeling rejection in the Black community for associating with the white community has caused me great pain. Denise's murder as my earliest memory seared into my consciousness that white people could hate me simply for being, but it didn't occur to me until I experienced it that I could also be hurt by my own people. I thought they were supposed to love and protect me. If I wasn't Black enough, I wish someone had taken me aside and shown me how to be more Black rather than criticizing me for something over which I had no control. If I'm being real, there were times growing up that I felt more comfortable with my white friends and wanted to reject my proud Black heritage, since I felt that's what some of my Black family and friends had done to me. To admit to these feelings is very embarrassing and comes with much shame. How could I feel the need to reject my own people? But the pain and discomfort was so great sometimes, it was more than I could bear.

Throughout my childhood and teen years, I found myself far more comfortable with white folks and white culture than with Black folks. My Caucasian friends were usually kinder to me while I was growing up. I fit in better there. It was always such an effort for me to be "Black." I never seemed to know the current slang or lingo; I never knew the music or the latest dances that most Black kids were doing. Even though I had one or two true friends who were Black, I didn't see them often. Early on, I made a decision to stay in that white world whenever possible. It was where I felt safe and comfortable. That was fine until the teen years and puberty came along, and the childlike nature of my young white friends gave way to the characteristics and attitudes of their white parents. The behavior that I first knew from white folks—that behavior that killed Denise—began to raise its ugly head. A white guy could be my friend at school, but he could never take me home to meet his mother and he would never date me or take me to the prom. My female friends would be polite, but somehow I just didn't fit in with them anymore. These were very lonely years. There was no joy in being with white *or* Black people.

The desire to reject my Blackness persisted for some time, but I eventually grew to know that thought process was unsustainable for the following two reasons. First, I was then and always will be Black. Second, I grew up under the legacy of my deceased older sister, Denise. Her portrait has always been displayed prominently in our home. It was and is a reminder that racial hatred in America can exist in lethal forms and that our family paid the ultimate price for that hatred. I could never turn my back on my people, even if I tried—because I am them, and they are me.

This book records my journey to discover who I am and how I gained peace with myself. I am exploring this through writing letters to the sister I never knew; the sister taken away from our family in such a tragic and senseless way. The struggles of my childhood and teenage years in an America that was not familiar to anyone I knew nonetheless might have been familiar to my older sister Denise, because she would have lived through some of the same struggles—had she been allowed to live. I had few people, either Black or white, to talk to about what I was feeling and even fewer who understood, but I could have and would have talked to her. No one had lived what I was living so that I could learn from their experiences. My parents, two of the most loving and supportive people in the world, could not help me because they didn't know anything about what I was going through. Mostly I didn't share with them because I knew they could not relate. Through many hurts, pains, and tears, I learned to make peace with both cultures around and inside of me. I want to write this book to help others who might be experiencing what I went through. To get past these feelings and to fully understand my identity, I am talking it through with Denise in these letters. In doing so, I hope to speak to those who have endured similar struggles and are still carrying around unexpressed pain because they didn't know there was anyone who shared their story and they decided to hate their own Blackness. It is my hope that by opening up and sharing my story, I can help others make this journey with less pain and more awareness and understanding. Maybe they won't have to go through what I did and they can love themselves; not some of themselves but all of their whole being. I want to be that older sister to them and share with them how I made my peace. I also want the world to be made aware of this part of life because I don't hear people speaking about it, at least not deeply or seriously. Maybe my book will begin the dialogue.

This collection of my letters to Denise also tells my life story and the story of our family after the horrific loss of my sister. I discuss how we have navigated through racism in this country. In these letters, I tell her about Mamma and Daddy, and what they have gone through, as best I know, since her death. I tell her that her life and death mattered not just to me, Mamma, Daddy, and our sister Kim, but to people she never knew. I wrote these letters over the course of many years, and since I started, some things have changed in my life and the lives of those closest to us. Some of our loved ones are no longer with us. I want her to understand that her people are not just her family, not just the ones she was in church with the day she died, not just people in Birmingham, not just people in Alabama, not just African Americans, not just Americans, but people throughout the world who truly appreciate the meaning of freedom and justice because she lived and died. That she was even important to the white people who were shamed by the tragedy of her death into taking a second look at the evils of segregation and what they needed to do to rectify it. And to the ones who were silent witnesses to the evil that was being perpetrated on our people and did not speak out about it.

I stand on the shoulders of my sister Denise, and as proud as I am to do so, I often wish I could have just cried on those shoulders while talking to her about school, about life, and about my dreams just one time.

Lisa S. McNair

Birmingham, Alabama

Sincere thanks for your lovely Gift

I was about 3 months old when this picture was taken. This was our Christmas card the year I was born. Mamma and Daddy must have sent a copy to everyone they knew. I don't think I have met any of their friends or family members who didn't have a copy of it. People would always pull it out and show it to us when we would stop by their homes. Photo by Chris McNair.

The Sister I Never Knew

Dear Denise,

I am your sister Lisa. I have so missed having a big sister all of my life. What makes your absence from my life so odd is that we never got to meet, and yet you are part of every aspect of my life. I can't tell you the number of times I wished you were alive and with us so that I could talk with you and know life having you as a big sister to me and Kim, our baby sister. I have so much to tell you.

I missed getting to know you, and have always wanted to talk to you and hug you. It is odd to lose a family member before meeting them, especially losing a sister, someone I would have grown up with, a partner and a sibling in this life. I can understand never meeting a grandparent, but not an older sister. It's so strange that I don't know what you sounded like or what your mannerisms were.

I was born almost exactly one year from the day of your death. Many people don't know that about our family's story. It's interesting how God works. How odd that Mamma and Daddy had not been able to bear more children after you were born. And yet after you were killed, they had two more little girls. I am the oldest child now and we have a younger sister named Kimberly who was born four years after I was, but I always wanted a big sister so I would have someone to talk to and look up to.

I think Mamma gave us all some beautiful names. I have always loved that Mamma gave you the first name Carol after her sister, whom she loved very much. I'm not sure why they didn't call you Carol, as Denise is your middle name. But that's the name that everyone knows you by. I wish I could have gotten to know and love you like Mamma loved her sister.

People ask me all the time, "When did you first know that your sister was killed in the bombing?" I can never answer that question definitively because it's something I have always known. I cannot recall a time when I didn't know about you and how you died. I guess people freely talked about it around me when I was a baby, and I just picked up on it. I am sure folks would see me with Mamma and say something like, "that is Maxine McNair. Her daughter was killed in the bombing and she was their only child, but now God has given them another baby." I don't ever recall someone sitting me down and telling me directly. And yet it is my first and oldest memory. It is a strange feeling to have a sister who died before you were born, especially in such a tragic and public way, and this feeling has been and always will be a part of who I am.

Your death thrust all of us, Mamma, Daddy, Kim, and me, into the surreal limelight of history. The bomb blast at 16th Street Baptist Church was heard all around the world and your death was a pivotal event in the Civil Rights Movement. People look at our family differently, treat us like celebrities sometimes, and put us on a pedestal. This all feels strange, even though it has been true for as long as I can remember. I am still not ever sure how to react to the attention. That is not how we see ourselves. We are just regular people who suffered an immense tragedy. When I first meet people, I don't say anything about you most of the time, but your death inevitably comes up. When I tell them you are my sister and how you died, most people are shocked and often sad and sorrowful. Others even burst into tears. It can be very emotional. How others experience the significance of your death is always quite moving for me. If I am with friends, they will usually bring it up. Close friends wait until I have left the room to bring it up or ask me first if it is okay to talk about you because they know I would rather someone get to know me for me first.

I have wanted to write and share my life with you as I would have done if you were not taken away from us so tragically. In recent years, God has placed several women in my life who are around the age you would have been, which is twelve years older than me. These women have been a source of great comfort to me. I can pretend that I do have a big sister and that in some ways you are with me through them. I can talk with them and learn what life might have been like back then for you. Many of them have their own memories of the day you were killed—where they were when it happened and how they felt when they learned the awful news.

The woman God sent to me whom I feel closest to is named Reena. Sadly, the Klan killed her father a few months before your murder. Reena's father's name was Medgar Evers. He lived in Mississippi and worked with the NAACP. He was well known for his fight for voting rights and became a target of the Klan. They assassinated him in his driveway one evening as he returned home. Reena and her brothers and mother ran out of their house when they heard the shots and saw him lying in a pool of blood, face down on the driveway. I can't even imagine that. She knows the pain of violent, senseless loss full well and I am sure it never leaves her.

The year 1963 was very sad for our country. Our president John F. Kennedy was also killed that year.

Her family's story, like ours, is well known. I find some solace in the fact that we share such a place of grief in such a public way. I can't share that with many people. She treats me as a friend but also mothers me a little, as I assume you would have. What binds me to Reena even more is that her middle name is Denise. When I learned that about her, I cried. She says I am the only person who calls her that. That has got to be a God thing. It is a very beautiful bond. You would like her very much. Maybe you have met her father up there in heaven. He would be very proud of her.

Many of those female mentors in my life tell me how their own mothers reacted at hearing the news of your death—most often with a sense of fear for their own children. Not all of these women are Black; several of them are white. I am sure they can't help but think about what it would have been like to die at church that day as they were also likely at their own houses of worship at the same time. In some ways, these women who were your peers relate to me as you and I would have as sisters. They love, support, and look out for me. They are a blessing from God.

One of the lines in your obituary was, "She received much joy from reading good books." I hope that will be true as you read this one. Surely you already know most of what I am telling you. I believe that people who die and go to heaven look down and see us. I pray that you all put in a good word of prayer for us in the presence of God, where you and the other girls surely went on that tragic day. I guess then that I am sharing not so much for your benefit but for my own and for anyone who will read these letters.

I love you and miss you,
Your Sister Lisa

Our Baby Sister

Dear Denise,

I want to tell you about our other sister, our little sister Kimberly. She has another wonderful name from Mamma. Mamma said that Daddy had another name in mind for her, but it was so bad she wouldn't let him use it (I think it was Thelma Selena). I remember when Kim was born and came home; it was the same year Dr. King was killed, 1968. I remember watching his funeral on TV with Mamma.

I was thrilled when Mamma and Daddy told me I was going to have a little brother or sister. However, I watched a lot of TV, and parents on TV always would give birth to a little boy if they already had a girl or a little girl if they already had a boy. So when Mamma brought home a baby girl, for the longest time I thought that there must have been a mistake. Surely, they needed to go back and get the little boy, I thought.

Growing up as the big sister was a new adventure. For four years I had been by myself. Mamma even said I had made up imaginary friends. Their names were Condi and Miller. Interestingly enough, my imaginary friends disappeared from my imagination as Kim grew up.

It has been interesting being the big sister. It wasn't always fun having a new sibling. I often wished you were here then. I thought if you were here she could have spent her time with both you and me. I felt I had to always look out for her and make sure she was all right. Probably because Mamma always said, "don't let anything happen to the baby, watch out for the baby, she's your responsibility." Even now as an adult I still worry about her.

I would say that Kim is more like Daddy than Mamma, although we each have some of their traits in us. Daddy is more carefree and artistic, and so is Kim. She has a very large personality and is very creative. Her first college degree was in fine arts painting from Auburn University. That makes life interesting: she went to Auburn and I went to the University of Alabama. Were you aware of the rivalry between those two schools when you were a child? Kim later went on to get two more degrees, one as a professional chef and another as a nutritional health coach. She now has her own catering business called Bitty's Living Kitchen.

This is the wedding party from Kim's wedding. We thought a lot about you that day and wished you were with us. From left to right: Kim's friends Terri Harris and Errica Williams, little miss Jamie Nealy (Kim's goddaughter), me, Kim, Pastor Gregory L. Clark, Jimmie Brock (your brother-in-law), Aric Jordan, little master Jalen William (Kim's godson), and Jared Brock and Ebbon Brock (Jimmie's brothers). Photo by Rick Streeter.

Kim loves to cook like Mamma. She is always in the kitchen creating new dishes. She is very much into vegan cooking and continues to educate herself in this culinary art. Often, people think of vegan food as being bland and tasteless, but not Kim's food—it is simply amazing. I love getting to be her taste-tester. She has mastered the art of making food we would normally prepare with meat taste just as good, if not better, without it. One Thanksgiving she made dressing, gravy, collard greens, and sweet potatoes with no animal fat whatsoever. They were amazingly delicious. Like other Thanksgiving meals, I ate so much that I could hardly move. She continues to create new dishes in this manner. I am very proud of her. She is living her dream.

Like you, as a child Kim had very long hair and was super skinny. Growing up, the biggest thing about her was her hair. She had a huge mane of it. It is very beautiful and jet-black. The strands are so thick. I envy her that a little. My hair is very soft and the strands are not nearly as thick and dark. I have always told her she was the pretty one and I was the smart one. She hates it when I say that. She has hands like Mamma. They both have the strongest and longest fingernails that grow naturally. Mine are short and brittle. I wonder what yours were like.

If you compare us to our grandmothers' personalities she is more like Dear Dear, our maternal grandmother, and I am more like Grandmother McNair. She

Kim and me at her wedding. I was her maid of honor. I was so moved that I cried all the way down the aisle. Kim was the first of us to get married, and Daddy walked her down the aisle. She had the best taste in her choice of flowers and decorations. It is still one of the most beautiful weddings I have ever attended. Photo by Rick Streeter.

is tall like Dear Dear and I am short like Grandmother McNair. Another way we are like them is that Dear Dear could have a very fiery personality while Grandmother McNair was often very soft-spoken and even-tempered.

Like many siblings, we have not always gotten along. We are very different people, as different as night and day, some say. I'll be honest and say I didn't really care much for her when we were children, and I am sure she felt the same way about me. However, a remarkable thing happened when I went off to college: She and I began talking on the phone. We shared news about our lives. She told me that she missed me, and our bond of sisterhood began to grow. We were no longer just sisters, but friends.

Kim has been married to a wonderful man named Jimmie Brock since 2005. She met him at church. He is a very sweet man and also very artistically talented. He is a musician and is originally from Mississippi. He has a delightful sense of humor. She is the first of us to marry. I hope to also, one day. They had a wonderful wedding. Kim didn't want a large wedding, but it was very beautiful. It was a fall wedding, celebrated in the evening and decorated with very warm autumn colors. It fit her personality. I always wanted to marry early in the morning in the spring when everything is new and beginning to grow. I want bright, vibrant colors in my wedding. Daddy walked her down the aisle and I cried the whole time. She came down the aisle in a custom-made dress and could not have looked more beautiful.

The wedding was held in her church, which was an old church with beautiful stained-glass windows. She only had three of us stand up with her. We wore brown dresses with gold accents and the men wore cream-colored tuxedos with ties to match the dresses. The bouquets were large with warm, rich colors: red and yellow flowers with dark green accents. The wedding was at 7:00 p.m. in December; it was dark outside, so she had beautiful candles lit in the windows. She wanted fall to resonate in what the guests saw but also in how the room smelled. She lit candles with rich cranberry and vanilla scents, and as you went downstairs to the reception there were candles that smelled of chocolate. It was a very warm and elegant experience. A "dessert reception" was held downstairs at the church and featured a wedding cake, small desserts, coffee, cocoa, and citrus-flavored water to balance all of the sweet treats. The biggest hit was the ice cream sandwiches made with Krispy Kreme doughnuts in a panini press. But it's at occasions like this that we can't help but miss you. I, of course, wonder whether you would have been married yourself; if your kids might have been the flower girl and the ring bearer at Kim's wedding. Mamma and Daddy looked great that day. It was a wonderful affair.

Kim and Jimmie moved in with Mamma and Daddy to help take care of them. They are in the same house you lived in, but it has now been remodeled twice since you lived in it. It is very beautiful and spacious but needs quite a few repairs. A house is quite a task to keep up. Nothing lasts forever.

I would have loved for you to have gotten to know Kim and now her husband. I would be fascinated to know what you and Kim liked and disliked about each other, and I can't help but think how my perspective on life would have been different if I had grown up as the middle sister instead of the big sister. We will all be together one day in heaven and we can't wait to meet you.

Peace and love my sister,

Lisa

Your Death Left Much Sorrow

Dearest Denise,

Your death left a lasting sorrow in our family and friends. It has been sad and sometimes hard to watch how it has affected them. I am still seeing the effects six decades later.

Mamma was, of course, the first person I saw go through the process of grieving you more than anyone. When I was younger she would cry often, sometimes for no apparent reason. I always figured it was over you. When we were little she would take us to your gravesite. Sometimes she would cry and sometimes she

At the top of this picture you can see Mamma and Daddy coming down
the stairs behind your casket. I find this simply heartbreaking.

would just stand and think. When she would weep it was the saddest sound anyone would want to hear. It was like a deep moaning, as if her sorrow was so far inside her and so very painful that it was too deep to ever heal. I have heard her cry like that so many times. It is a sound that haunts my mind and will never go away. I saw some newsreel footage of people leaving the sanctuary on the steps of the church after your funeral. There were hundreds of people and many people crying. And although I could not see Mamma, I could hear her crying over all of the others. It was heartbreaking. Often, she would cry at home but many times it was when we were at church. As a child, when people would cry in church over a song or something the preacher might say, adults would say "they are just happy," crying from a feeling of joy or affirmation. Well, there was nothing happy about Mamma's tears. They were from a place of deep grief and sadness. It was a loss no one could fill.

As the years went on she cried less, at least in our presence. She stopped taking us to the cemetery around the time I was in middle school, but she would still go herself. I would go too sometimes, once I began driving. I would just stop by to talk to you, always wondering what it would really be like to have a conversation with you.

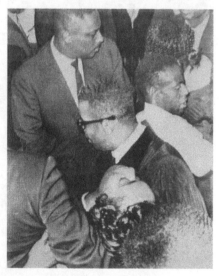

Someone shared this photo of Mamma with me on Facebook. It is of Mamma at the cemetery. She was literally overcome with grief, and she passed out. It is hard to imagine her pain: to bury your only child, your beautiful little girl. I don't know how she survived it.

I don't know if or when Daddy ever went by your gravesite, except for the few times he went with us. Daddy has always been less forthcoming about his emotions. He is from that generation of men who don't know how—or aren't willing—to show emotions. They often felt that they should remain stoic. Relatives have told me that it was more than six months after you died that he cried out loud for the first time. That is so hard for me to imagine. He would tell me that he decided to go into public office as his way of dealing with what happened to you. He believed in our legal system even though it had not always been fair to our people.

However, I know he still grieved. Sometimes I would catch him having a faraway look, particularly around your birthday or the anniversary of your murder. He never forgot you and his hurt never went away. Many, many years later there was a documentary made about you and the other girls by a famous Black filmmaker by the name of Spike Lee. After Spike and Daddy had their initial conversation about the film, he came to visit us and talk about it. It was his first time making a documentary and he did a fine job. Once he found out that Daddy was a professional photographer, that he had a treasure trove of photographs chronicling your whole life, and that Mamma and Daddy had kept all of your things in trunks in the garage, he was mesmerized and very excited. He asked that we gather all the pictures we could find and all of your things, and he would fly back to town to look at them and start making the film.

Well, by this time things in our house had been moved around quite a bit during remodels. There were pictures and things of yours in a number of closets all over the house. Mamma and I got right on the task we were assigned, pulling pictures and your personal effects. It was a sad time. We did have a few moments of laughter as well. Mamma had stories about lots of things we found. It was good to do that with her. We had hoped that Daddy would help and be a part of that process. I looked forward to hearing stories from him, but he always managed to be too busy to help us. It made me and Mamma angry that we were doing all the work. One day when we were going through a particular closet he was home all day, which was rare. We asked him to please help us. He sat down for a little while and then shortly afterwards got up to leave. I asked him how he could leave us with all of that to do and he yelled back at me, "I just can't!" He had tears in his eyes. Mamma touched my shoulder and told me to leave him alone. That was the first time I had seen him cry over you. He had held all that hurt and pain in for so many years and never dealt with it. I felt so bad for him. I later went in his room and gave him a hug and apologized for fussing at him. It broke my heart to see him like that, but I was glad he was finally grieving.

Once the documentary was released there were many premieres all over the country. Kim and I went to two of the premieres, but Mamma and Daddy went to all of them and cried at every single one. I guess Daddy was finally free to grieve.

When I think of those who were saddened by your death, I can't forget Lynn, our first cousin. You and she were the best of friends, two sisters' first-born girls, only a couple of years apart. According to Mamma you were inseparable, you did everything together. I know that to be true because there are so many pictures of the two of you together. Mamma said that the only reason Lynn wasn't killed that day too was that our cousin Nedric, Lynn's little brother and just a baby, was sick that day, so Auntie Nee Nee, Mamma's sister, didn't go to church and neither did her children.

Lynn's sorrow over your death is difficult for me to imagine. Like Daddy, she kept her grief inside. I think about the tools that are offered now for such tragedies that weren't offered then. When there is a horrible incident today like the bombing or a shooting at a church or a school, lots of folks come to the rescue. Where kids are involved, counselors are immediately dispatched to give comfort and counsel to the grieving children. But none of that happened when you were killed. I have talked to so many folks who were kids back then and who knew the girls. They said they all went back to school on Monday, the day after the bombing, like nothing ever happened. Many adults I know didn't talk about it either. There was a whole culture of silence that went on for decades. As Black people in this country we knew that nothing would happen to white men who killed a Black person. So, although there was an investigation immediately following the murders and five men were immediately identified, no one was brought to justice and the case was put on a shelf.

Sadly, this was devastating for Lynn. I don't think anyone talked to her about how she was feeling and the grief she had experienced. I always loved Lynn a lot and looked up to her as I would have you. She was the closest thing I had to you. She was fun to be around. As a child she would paint my fingernails and let me wear her high heels around the house. They were of course too big for me, but I could pretend I was a "big girl" like Lynn. As I grew, I wanted more than anything to ask her about you, but whenever I did she would cleverly distract me and change the subject. Much time passed before I realized that she just didn't want to talk about it and I would never get answers from Lynn to my questions. I later thought how smart she was not to say she didn't want to talk about you. She knew that would be a red flag and I would have pressed her even harder.

I will never forget that when Spike Lee came to visit after we had gathered all of your things and all of your photos, he noticed Lynn in more than half of the pictures of you. He asked who she was and wanted to speak with her. We told him that she had never spoken about you and most probably would not speak with him. He was determined and asked to speak with her. She lived in California at the time, so we called her and let Spike talk with her. He asked her if she would talk about you, and she told him yes. He agreed to fly her and her son home to be interviewed. He bought them tickets to Birmingham. We were very excited to get to see them but also to finally hear her thoughts about your death. Sadly, she never picked the tickets up and never was interviewed by him. I would have loved to hear what she would have said about you. I think it would have been good for her to let go of some of her grief. I hate that she didn't feel strong enough to do it.

Sadly, Lynn's life didn't end well. She had suffered for years with alcoholism and, I am sure, undiagnosed depression. She had trouble holding down a job. It was always nice when she came home but she was a shell of a person. I don't know if any of us really knew her. When she drank she was silly and loud, but I never recall having any meaningful conversations with her. Later we learned that she had problems with drugs as well. They eventually killed her. When she died I was so angry with her for dying like that. It seemed so senseless. Then I thought about it: She most likely suffered from survivor's guilt. She would have been with you that day if she had gone to church, and she was never the same after that. When she died, I felt empty. Like I never really knew her. I felt that she had never really lived. Then I realized, she didn't—because the real Lynn died on September 15, 1963, when you did, and likely never learned how to live again.

Your death didn't just affect friends and family members but also our city, state, country, and world. The people of Wales were very moved by your death. All the way across the pond, as they say. They were so moved that they dedicated a large stained-glass window to you and the other girls. I learned of this later. What was most interesting about it is that the window did not come from the Welsh government or the royal family but from individual citizens of Wales. Individuals raised money in small increments to have this window made for you. They found an artist and paid for the window to be flown here and installed at 16th Street. It is a very beautiful window with the image of Jesus on a cross, and Jesus is Black.

At the bottom of the window it has the words "YOU DO IT TO ME," which is paraphrasing Christ's words that "if you do this to the least of these, you do it unto me." I just love this window and what it means. I would love to personally thank the people of Wales and hope to travel there one day.

Our family members weren't the only ones who felt your loss. Many friends of yours and ours have only recently begun to express how the girls' deaths affected them. Every time someone shares their story with me, we cry together. It is so sad that we felt for decades that those feelings could not be expressed. One of my friends from 16th Street recently told me she was one of the children who was injured by the flying glass on that day. I have known her all my life and only long after we were adults did she mention it. Your death along with the other girls is etched in all of our souls here in Birmingham and beyond. You will never be forgotten.

I'll never forget you,
Lisa

This stained-glass window, designed by artist John Petts, was donated by the citizens of Wales in memory of you and the other girls. It was flown here and installed in 1965. It is a very large window in the back of the sanctuary, in the balcony. It is simply breathtaking. I always thought it was amazing that people from the other side of the world also felt the pain of that day. Photo by Audra Gray.

What a Difference a Year Makes

Dear Denise,

I have told you that I was born almost a year to the day after you were murdered. I can only imagine the excitement that Mamma and Daddy felt at my birth. The entire Birmingham community was happy for them because—as I have already told you—our parents had difficulties having babies. That is why you were an only child. They had a number of miscarriages between each of us (and one stillbirth). I know folks who were close to them were thrilled for Mamma and Daddy when I arrived, knowing both the struggles they had been through and that you were their only child at the time of your death at age eleven. I often meet women Mamma's age or older who say to me, "You are here! Thank God! We prayed for you." I even appeared in *Jet* magazine as a baby.

I like to think that you had a happy life during your short time here with our parents, grandparents, uncles, cousins, and close friends, even though you all lived in the Jim Crow South. Because of the circumstances surrounding your death, and even though I was the second child, I was treated like a first child. I was given huge amounts of attention and love, especially from our extended family. You were the first grandchild on both sides of our family, so I am sure you were smothered with love and attention too.

We were blessed with wonderful grandparents, all of whom are with you now in heaven. Mamma's parents, Dear Dear and Granddaddy Mac, were awesome. Their real names were Clara Marshall Pippen and Maxell Pippen. I don't remember Granddaddy Mac because he passed away while I was quite young, but Mamma has always filled our lives with interesting stories about him. She told us that he had a great sense of humor and was always teasing people and cracking jokes. I love the fact that he was a successful business owner and did very well for his family. Mamma said that Granddaddy Mac's business, Social Cleaners, was a dry cleaning store that had pick-up locations all over town. He went to trade school and was a very smart man.

Dear Dear, our maternal grandmother, was the rock of our family. All things revolved around her, and she was a *strong* Black woman. If she said it, that settled

¶ **A Memorial:** Before Lisa McNair was born, her sister, Carol, was one of four girls murdered in racist bombing of Birmingham's Sixteenth Street Baptist Church. Lisa sits before $2,000 stained glass window of brown Jesus Christ donated to church by the people of Wales.

31

I have lived in the public eye from the very beginning. This is a picture of me from *Jet* magazine at the unveiling of the stained-glass window that the people of Wales donated to 16th Street and the families of the bombing victims. I was not yet a year old.

it, and there was no discussion. I was always impressed that she had a college degree from Alabama State University. Did you know that? It was quite a feat for a Black woman to get a college degree back then. Most of my friends have parents who have degrees, but not grandparents. Mamma said that Dear Dear taught school and even helped found a school. I loved her very much. She was always there when we needed her and taught us about how to put some money away for a "rainy day," as she called it. I never knew her to be broke.

She told us an interesting story about how she started her first savings account. As she recalled, Granddaddy Mac liked to party and he would go out drinking. Some nights he would go out and have a little too much to drink, and it really angered her. One night he came home drunk, and he pulled off his pants and laid them on the bedroom floor. He fell asleep and, when he did, she went into his pockets and took a few dollars. She told us, "That's how I started my savings account. He never missed it because he was so drunk that he never remembered how much he had spent." She said I should always have some money of my own, especially when I got married, "because you never know what will happen." I do that now, even though I am not married yet. You never know when an emergency will arise.

Dear Dear helped keep our family together. If one member of the family did something, we all came out to support it. If one of us kids were in a play or had a solo at church, a speech, or a sporting event, she would make sure that everyone in the family attended.

I love this photo of Mamma and me shortly after I was born. She looks so happy, but I know she is thinking about you. Photo by Chris McNair.

While I was in elementary school, she came to live with us part-time—during the weekdays, mostly during the school year—to help Mamma get us ready for school and with household chores. Daddy was gone a lot then, traveling to Montgomery three days a week to serve in the legislature. It was great having Dear Dear live with us. We would leave for school and when we came back, she would have made our beds up, placing our stuffed animals on top and leaving pieces of candy by them. We were always excited to find the candy, which she said the stuffed animals had purchased for us when they went out shopping. I thought that was such a cute thing to say. We all knew that she had put the candy there. She was so loving.

I would love to hear your memories of Granddaddy Mac, whom I'm sure you knew well. And of course, you would have had your own stories about Dear Dear and life with Mamma and Daddy. I've got so much more to tell you.

Much love,
Your Sister Lisa

Our Lineage Is a Strong One

Dear Denise,

It is clear to me that we come from a good long line of strong, wise, tough, and resilient people. I am proud of our parents, who brought us into the world, and I know you are too. Our father's name is unusual—Jewel Christopher McNair—and he married our mother, who also has a special name, Thelma Maxine Pippen McNair. I like to tease them both that they are living under aliases because neither one of them uses their first name. They have gone by Chris and Maxine all of my life; I wonder if they did when you were alive. I have always wanted to ask our grandparents how they came up with Mamma's and Daddy's first names. Our grandfather's name was also Jewel McNair—not Jewel Christopher but just Jewel McNair. Our parents were born to parents who had a great deal of pride and self-respect, and that was passed down to their children and to us.

As you know, our father hails from a little town in Arkansas called Fordyce. What you may not know is that another person of note who came from there was Coach Paul "Bear" Bryant, a famous football coach at the University of Alabama. Did you ever hear of "The Bear?" He is a legend around these parts, even among Black folks. When he began coaching at Alabama there were no Black players on the team's roster. Alabama desegregated its football team in 1971 and went on to win three more national championships under Coach Bryant, which gave him six national titles—a record that was only matched by another Alabama coach, Nick Saban, the current football coach at Alabama. Once Alabama accepted both Black and white players on its team it has had equally passionate fans of all races. However, it was said that there was a time that Coach Bryant didn't want Black players on his team. I understand that he came to change his ways and regretted that attitude. Although there are a whole lot of Bama fans of color, there are still quite a few who will not root for the Tide because of his past attitude toward Black people. I am not one of them. I attended the University of Alabama and have fond memories of my time there.

Granddaddy McNair, as we grandkids called him, was a strong, proud individual like many African American men of that time. He lived on a hundred-acre farm that he bought in Arkansas in the late 1920s or early 1930s. I marvel that a Black man in his day was able to earn enough money to purchase that much land, not to mention that he was allowed to purchase land from the white establishment in the Jim Crow South. It gives me a sense of pride that we were related to such a man. It makes me feel like we resembled the fictional family depicted on the television series *Dallas*. The grandfather in that show was a man with a great deal of pride who had built a business dynasty for himself and his family from nothing, just like our grandfather. This show was a huge hit and was on television for many years after your death. Mamma, Kim, and I watched it every week without fail. We would plan our evening around it and make sure we were home to watch it together. If anyone would call us on the phone we would get really upset and look at each other and wonder, "who in the world would be calling us at this time? Don't they know that *Dallas* is on?"

Television was a big part of my early life. Did you watch much television? What were your favorite shows? You would not believe how television has changed today, and how many Black people are featured on the multitude of channels we now have. I guess you only had three or four channels back then, but we have hundreds now! The pictures are all in vivid color with no static or antennas to adjust. We have come a long way. The televisions are very large too, some are as large as eighty inches wide. I know that must be hard to believe.

Of course, Granddaddy McNair did not have millions of dollars, but having that land made him an important man in his town of Fordyce among Black people as well as white. I am sure you visited Granddaddy and Grandmother McNair in Arkansas. I have, but it's been a while since we have been there. I love going there and touching the soil that is our legacy from Granddaddy McNair. Several years ago, Daddy had a house built on the land for our family. One of our uncles and his wife live in Grandma and Granddaddy's house there too.

Perhaps you remember that our grandfather had twelve children with Grandmother McNair—nine boys and three girls—and he ruled his family with an iron hand. Is that how you remember him? That did not always endear him to me. I always wanted him to loosen up and show some genuine emotion and not be so stern all the time. I guess that just wasn't the way of Black men at that time. They had to cover up their emotions around white people and because they had so little control over things, I guess they had to boss someone. I imagine Black men of his generation often didn't have much to laugh or be happy about.

Grandmother McNair was a jewel. Her full name was Lillie Bell Childs McNair. She was the sweetest and most God-fearing person I ever met. She was kind and soft-spoken. Several family members say I remind them of her because, like her, I am not a very tall woman. Grandmother didn't work outside of the home. Because of all the children she had, she had a ton of grandchildren; I believe there are thirty-four of us. However, she remembered all of our birthdays. She would always send me a card or write me a letter and include five dollars. That had to be tough for her because they didn't have much money. I remember she did that for years for all of the grandkids. She would always say to me, "be a good girl."

For many people, when they refer to grandmothers they often talk about their good cooking. I can't really say that about either of our grandmothers. Our grandmother Dear Dear, who is our Mother's mom, would always take us to a soul food restaurant after church. I really don't recall her cooking anything memorable—she cooked but it wasn't much to write home about. I do remember that some Thanksgivings she would make dressing with oysters in it. Now *that* was good. When I saw Grandmother McNair it was usually in Arkansas and there were lots of aunties around who did the cooking while we were there. The only thing I know she made that I loved were her pear preserves that she made from the pear orchard that is on the land there on our family's property. Her pear preserves on hot-from-the-oven biscuits were delicious, and I can taste them still in my imagination. Daddy learned to make the biscuits and one year made the preserves. They were just like hers. I wish I knew how to make those preserves and had some now.

Mamma and Daddy struggled with health problems as they got older. We hired some wonderful caregivers to help with their care. One of Mamma's caregivers is our neighbor Ethel. You played with her as a child. I take care of all their bills. We all lived together until I moved out for the first time when I turned fifty! In your day, Black people could never have lived in some of the buildings or neighborhoods I have. For several years, I lived in a high-rise condo in the historic Southside district of Birmingham. I wish you could have seen my place. It has the best view of Birmingham and I loved it. I was on one of the upper floors and could see all of downtown Birmingham and beyond. My neighbors were great. Interestingly enough, while I was there, only three other Black residents lived in the building. It wasn't discrimination, but I think folks just didn't know about it. Whenever one of these units goes on the market it is rarely there more than a few short days.

You helped make desegregation possible because your death caused people to realize how crazy segregation was. The ways of the Jim Crow South didn't die right away, but they gradually disappeared so that now we can live pretty much wherever we want, which I consider a blessing. I wonder where you would live if you were alive today. I wonder if you would have left Birmingham as many of your generation did. It was so hard to live here. Many left and never came back. Some are coming back now after having been away for more than fifty years. If you stayed here, I hope you would live close by where I live and not out of town. If you did live out of town, however, it would be fun to take a road trip to visit you.

Much love,
Your Sister Lisa

School Days

Dear Denise,

Going to school had changed when I came along. I went to different schools than you did. Mamma said you attended Center Street School. She taught there and took you with her every day even though you weren't zoned to attend there. I first started elementary school at Roosevelt Elementary School, which was the only elementary school in the small municipality called Roosevelt City where we lived. Its claim to fame was that it was the only city in Alabama at the time run by all African American leadership. Sometime in the 1980s, Roosevelt City was annexed into Birmingham because Birmingham was a much larger city and could offer better services like fire and police protection due to its much larger tax base. Many of our neighbors didn't want the city to annex our neighborhood because they liked that our community was all Black, but sadly it lacked the tax base, which didn't allow for the provision of basic services like fire protection with a full-time fire station; nor did we have a full-time police force, just to name two issues. There weren't any white students at Roosevelt Elementary School from what I can remember. There were a few white teachers, but all the students were Black.

I would like to explain something to you. You may see me use the term "Black" to describe us. You may have been familiar with that term. However, some years after your death we began to call ourselves African American. This is because we are of African descent. Some Black people still prefer to use the term "Black" as opposed to African American. I actually like African American because of its descriptive nature. However, being called Black does not bother me.

First grade was a wonderful experience. My teacher was Mrs. Kennedy, a Black woman who taught me a great deal. In those days, you were a person of status if you were a teacher, especially in the Black community. It seemed as if the Black teachers back then all knew each other, at least those who taught in Jefferson County, Alabama. That was one indication of how close-knit our community was. Since Mamma was a teacher, she was acquainted with Mrs. Kennedy and knew she was an excellent teacher.

I was eager and willing to learn, and she was kind and helpful to all the students. Mamma didn't stop teaching when she left her classroom and would continue to teach me things when she got home from work. At this time, Mamma was teaching third grade at Jones Valley Elementary School. I did not go to school with her. I asked her one day why we couldn't go to school with her. She told me that she took you with her and said she would never do that with Kim and me. I guess it made her sad.

In those days, I was always ahead of the class, so I could help my classmates when I finished my work and I enjoyed doing so. I remember that Mamma taught me cursive writing. I loved it. However, students in public schools were not supposed to learn that skill until the second grade. When I used it in Mrs. Kennedy's first grade class she asked me not to because the other students didn't know it yet.

I'm sure you remember how Mamma woke us up each morning for school. When I think of things like this, I know you had a good life. She would sing the "Good Morning to You" song in that melodious, classically trained voice she has. Looking back, I remember it as being the sweetest thing. Do you remember the words?

> Good morning to you.
> Good morning to you.
> We're all in places
> With bright shiny faces.
> For this is the way
> To start our new day!

If we didn't respond right away, she would continue to gently chide us to get us up. Finally, if none of her efforts worked, Daddy would come into our room and, with his booming voice, he would crow like a rooster. That would get us out of bed with giggling and laughter. Sometimes we stayed in bed just so Daddy would have to come in and do his rooster call.

I enjoyed going to school every day. Mamma would always put me in cute little dresses with bows and ribbons in my hair; I think I saw pictures where she did the same for you. I even wore some of your dresses. Your clothes and the ones she bought me were always so adorable. When she had time, she would make us new dresses. That was mostly for special occasions like Easter or Christmas. I remember one dress of yours had a plaid design and it was really cute. Mamma dressed me up to have my picture made with that one. Mamma loved dressing us up. I was too young to use perfume but instead of baby powder, Mamma would buy dusting powder in the fragrance of the perfume she wore. With the very dainty powder puff that came with it she would give me a pat of powder on my chest and back before she put on my clothes. Both Kim and I always smelled and looked like pretty little dolls.

After she dressed me for school, she always gave me forty cents for lunch every day—one quarter, one nickel, and one dime tied neatly in a handkerchief. One day she gave me eight nickels, which was not what I was used to. When I arrived at school and opened the handkerchief, I was upset. I had not learned to count money yet, and I assumed I was not going to be able to eat lunch because I didn't have the right number of coins.

This is one of my favorite pictures from my childhood. It is a picture of me the year I started first grade. I believe Mamma told me that I am wearing one of your dresses. She always dressed us up like pretty little dolls. Photo by Chris McNair.

I was trying to be a big girl and not cry but Mrs. Kennedy noticed something was wrong when I didn't line up for lunch with the other students. When she came over to me and asked what was wrong, I did begin to cry. Through my tears, I told her I was going to have to miss lunch because Mamma had not given me the correct money. I opened my handkerchief and showed her the coins. She sweetly put her arms around me and informed me that what I had was just right, and then began teaching me the values of the coins I had been given. I was so relieved. I did not think Mamma would have made such a mistake, but I just didn't understand. Mrs. Kennedy was the consummate teacher and a very kind and loving person.

That first-grade year was also when I met Wendy Sykes. Wendy's mother and Mamma taught together at the same school for a while, and that is how they came to know each other. Wendy and I got along very well together. Our mothers were very down-to-earth and there were similarities in the ways they raised us, so we played well together. Her father was a coach at Roosevelt Elementary School and she came to school with him every day.

Wendy and I grew to be close friends. Our mothers would take us to each other's homes to play. Then they taught us how to write letters to each other so we could communicate and stay in touch. It seems silly now when I realize that we only lived seven or eight minutes from each other and both our homes had telephones. I guess that was the teacher in each of them, making sure we developed good writing skills. Wendy's father was transferred to another school the summer after our first-grade year so Wendy didn't come back to Roosevelt the next year. I missed having her around every day. We have maintained our friendship to this day, and I am now, proudly, the godmother to her sons.

In the second grade, I was assigned my first white teacher. I wasn't sure about having a white teacher at first, and I am sure that my fellow classmates felt the same. It had been only a few years since many Civil Rights incidents, including your death. Black and white people had just begun to associate with each other. There was such a bad history between our two races that many of us had trouble trusting white people because doing so had not always turned out well. That being said, she made us all feel welcome and at ease right away. She was a very kind person and made us laugh. She also was a very good teacher and I grew to love her. She took time to give each of us individual attention, and she embraced my desire to excel in school. I was not unfamiliar with white people. Our father's pastor was a white man and his family was around us a good bit. Sadly, before the first semester of that year was over, my teacher was transferred to another school, and we had to merge our class with another second-grade class.

I was devastated. She told us of her departure early that morning and I tried to be strong, but by the end of that school day, I was inconsolable. One of my classmates was a friend and neighbor, Roderick Woods, who lived a couple of blocks from me and had also been in my first-grade class. Roderick had a schoolboy crush on me and always teased me. When I left the school building every day, he would take the hat off my head (Mamma dressed us in hats for school when the weather was cold) and I would chase him around the schoolyard to get it back. He was a lot of fun even though he stole my hat every day.

Roderick felt sorry for me because I couldn't stop crying. He consoled me by putting his arm around me, but then he began to cry because he liked our teacher too. While we were doing all that crying, we missed the school bus home. It was late fall at this time and the sun had begun to go down. We must have been outside for a very long time. Our teacher came outside as she was about to leave for the day and saw how upset we were, and came over to comfort us. She realized we had missed the bus and would have to make the long walk home in the cold. She graciously offered to take us both home in her car. I am not sure that would happen today. Today, children have to send in a list of approved people who are allowed to pick them up at the beginning of each year. I remember thinking how nice it was for her to do that. I wish I could remember her name. I would like to find her and see what she is doing now and thank her again for being so kind.

The next school day our class merged with the other second grade class, which also was taught by a white woman. She was very different from my original second grade teacher. From that point on I learned almost nothing for the rest of the year. Our new teacher, Mrs. Shelley, appeared upset and angry to be there and didn't seem to care if we learned anything or not. In my mind, she came across as nothing more than an overpaid babysitter. I was the kind of child who enjoyed the challenge of learning new things, and not to be taught anything was unsettling.

The one assignment I do remember completing over and over again was writing sentences. However, we weren't being creative and crafting our own sentences; instead, we were just copying words off the chalkboard. Mrs. Shelley would write sentences on the board and leave a blank line somewhere in the sentence for us to fill in a word. At the end of the sentence, after the period, she would draw a picture. That was the word we needed to fill in the blank. I know she showed us a picture of a whale a million times. If I live to be one hundred years old, I'll never forget how to spell *whale*.

In the last part of class, we would watch television for a good bit of the day, especially public television. I wonder if you know what public television is and I'll bet you can't imagine watching TV in school. We were watching the television one day and witnessed Governor Wallace being shot. He was also the governor when you were living. He was famous for saying "segregation now, segregation tomorrow, and segregation forever!" Seeing him shot on TV was quite shocking. Needless to say, there were mixed feelings about him being shot, as he had not been nice to Black people in Alabama.

I learned as early as second grade that there were some nice white folks and some not-so-nice ones—they all weren't the same. However, I could not help but notice that not all my classmates had that same thought. Many of them lumped all the white people into one group and called them all "bad." Considering our racial history in this country, I understand why. But our family's association with Daddy's white pastor and the first teacher I had in the second grade allowed me not to paint all white folks with the same brush.

Mrs. Shelley never seemed to want to interact with us at all; therefore, we were not naturally drawn to her. Many of my classmates didn't like her either, but mostly because she was white. I wanted to like her as I had liked the previous teacher but the peer pressure from my classmates was just too strong. Rarely have I conformed to peer pressure in my life, but that was one of those rare times when I followed the behavior of those around me. Most of my life, I have been my own person, but this time I followed the lead of others and I am not proud of it. It was an awful year.

Most of the time we didn't sit at individual desks but at six-foot tables with chairs around them. A mean little girl named Harriett ruled the table where I sat. Everyone at that table was terrified of her, and we followed her lead out of fear. She was the first true bully I knew. Harriett hated the teacher and wanted all of us to hate her too. She was disrespectful to the teacher and wanted us to follow suit. I came close to doing some of the things she asked us to do, but I knew I couldn't behave too badly because when it got back to Mamma, there would be hell to pay.

Mamma gave all my teachers, even through my freshman year in high school, the same speech every year: "If Lisa cuts up, you beat her behind, then call me, and I will beat her again when she gets home." She knew she had taught me how to behave in public and expected nothing less than exemplary behavior. She probably told your teachers the same thing. Mamma's spankings were no fun, and I was determined to stay out of trouble, Harriett or no Harriett.

Harriett taught me some important lessons, and I will tell you about some of them in another letter. I would love to know what school was like for you, who your teachers were, what you loved and disliked the most, your fondest and happiest and strangest memories. In a life cut short like yours, I feel sure that every single day is a treasure.

Love,
Your Sister Lisa

Have Mamma and Daddy Gone Crazy?

Dear Denise,

I wrote to you about my classmate Harriett and promised to tell you more. Harriett had a dark brown complexion. Her skin was the color of dark chocolate. Although everyone likes chocolate that color, in a Black person it was not always looked at favorably. She was so obsessed with her coloring that she made it a topic at our second-grade table every day. Evidently, someone had made fun of the color of her skin, as if it wasn't beautiful because it was dark. She hated her complexion and was self-conscious about it. I hated the fact that she had been made to hate her color. I wish she knew that all shades of Black are beautiful. The different shades that we come in as African Americans have always been an issue with us, and I'm sure it was the same when you were growing up.

Harriett made us all participate in a strange test once a week. We would lay our hands in the middle of the table and see who was getting lighter. Of course, none of our skin tones were changing, but Harriett swore that her skin was. That reflected the common but unfortunate thinking among African Americans that it was preferable to be a lighter-skinned Black person than one with darker skin. Another of Harriett's tests about our racial identity involved holding our lips in so they wouldn't seem so large, because having large lips was not necessarily seen as a good thing back then.

As Black children, we were taking on some of the self-loathing that white culture had helped to create through stereotypes dating back to the times of slavery and that is still prevalent in our culture today. The self-loathing may have lessened, but it has never left us completely. What is funny now is that white folks consider full lips sexy and are having them cosmetically enlarged. Who knew?

As you might have guessed, I was glad when the second grade ended and summer arrived. I wasn't looking forward to going back for the third grade, especially if Harriett was going to be in my class. Little did I know that our parents didn't want me in public school any longer and had been trying for several years to get me into an excellent, almost exclusively white private school in downtown Birmingham.

I vaguely remember going downtown with Daddy to take an entrance exam at a place called Advent Episcopal Day School. The folks at Advent told Mamma and Daddy that I didn't pass the test to get in years earlier when they wanted me to enter that school as a four-year-old for kindergarten. Mamma and Daddy had a hard time not believing that racism rearing its ugly head was the reason I didn't get in the first time they tried. How can someone not be smart enough for four-year-old kindergarten? After all, Mamma had always taught me at home to complement what I was learning at school.

Daddy is a persistent man when he wants something, so he tried again to get Kim and me into Advent during my second-grade year at Roosevelt Elementary. This time the school told him that my sister and I could be admitted. Kim, who was three at the time, was permitted to start four-year-old kindergarten before her fourth birthday. Advent told our parents that I needed to repeat the second grade. They felt that I didn't have the knowledge required to do the work, and they were afraid I would start off third grade behind the other children. Daddy kept insisting that I be placed in the third grade, but Mamma agreed with the folks at Advent. I wasn't too upset because I knew, even at that young age, that I had not learned anything my second year at Roosevelt. Although it was tough to tell my friends I had to repeat the second grade, it was actually a pretty smooth transition. Since I was not going to be in school with friends from my neighborhood, that lessened the stigma of repeating a grade. Daddy was happy nonetheless when I was admitted. I guess it was his way of realizing "the Dream" for us, as someone who had lived most of his life, up to that point, in the Jim Crow South, which came with much oppression and few opportunities. He probably felt he could not give you all you needed but was determined to give those things to Kim and me.

When Mamma and Daddy informed me that I would be switching schools, I was happy at first because I was not looking forward to another year of being bullied by Harriett. But when they told me it was the white school where I had taken that test, I was terrified. As a small child, I didn't have the insight to see what was occurring. I couldn't imagine why our parents wanted to send me to Advent. They had lost you to the hands of white racists, and they were sending us both to a school that was almost exclusively white and that wasn't even in our neighborhood. It was too far to walk home if there was a problem at school: Advent was at least thirty minutes from our home by car. I wouldn't know who to talk to if I encountered hate at school.

As a seven-year-old, I knew I was Black, of course, and felt as if white people, for the most part, harbored racial hatred for me. It didn't help that the school was only four blocks away from 16th Street Baptist Church. I remembered seeing only white people when Daddy took me down to Advent. They assured us that everything was going to be just fine. They even mentioned that there was another Black student enrolled at Advent who would be in my class, and that I should look for her. Despite these reassurances, I was still terrified!

Had they forgotten that white folks kill Black folks? I didn't know any of the people at Advent. I don't remember expressing any of these thoughts and emotions to our parents because I had always been an obedient child. In those days, children did as they were told. Not so much today. Many children are allowed to be disrespectful and talk back to their parents. I did what our parents said and didn't argue with them. They assured me that Advent would work out fine and that I would enjoy my new school. Even though they tried to assure me, I was still leery of their decision, and I still wondered if something was wrong with them. I learned years later that Mamma was not really in favor of us attending Advent. She was also afraid, for the same reasons that I was, but she never let on. Also, because Advent was a private school Mamma and Daddy had to pay a good bit of money for us to attend there. I wasn't sure if you knew that about private schools. Public schools are free for anyone to attend. Mamma was the main breadwinner at the time and I am sure she was concerned about being able to afford to send us there. Also, she was a public-school teacher and didn't think it would be bad for us to attend public schools. She knew so many teachers in Birmingham and knew they worked hard to give students a good education.

I didn't know what was wrong with our parents. People said they loved me, but it was time to stick up for myself because those two had obviously gone crazy! After pondering this situation for a while, I knew I had to come up with a rationale that would give me peace of mind, because I didn't want to disappoint Mamma and Daddy. I finally decided I should give this new school a try to see what it was like, but that I would watch my back the whole time. Although I am not a violent person by nature and was admonished by Mamma not to get into fights at school or anywhere else, as a child I thought that if any white person tried to kill me, beat me up, or harm me in any way, I would not go down without a fight. If any white person tried to assault me, they were going down with me.

Later I found out that my fears were unwarranted, because Advent was the first private school to integrate in the state of Alabama. From my second grader's perspective, it was scary stuff at the time. I can't wait to tell you about my experiences at Advent. It's late, though, already. And I have to rest for a long day of work tomorrow, so more to follow just as soon as I can.

Much love,
Lisa

Not So Bad

Dear Denise,

I recently went back to Advent after many years and I am astounded by how it has changed. Today, the student body is composed of 25 percent students of color. When we were there that number was less than 5 percent. The South has changed, Denise, and you would not recognize it if you came back today. In some ways, your death helped make racial conditions better. Mamma tells a story about you asking if you could march for freedom in Birmingham during the Children's Crusade in 1963, and she told you that you were too young. Little did she know that your death would be pivotal in the struggle for justice, more than your protest marching ever could.

This is my second-grade class at Advent. It was my first year there. I am on the first row, third from the left. The photographer said something funny and I was trying not to laugh when the photo was taken. Courtesy of the author.

The first day of class at Advent was scary. I didn't know what to expect, but I had my guard up. Mamma had chosen a pretty dress for me that morning, as she always did, and had given me her usual speech about how to behave. She always told us to be on our best behavior and not to embarrass her in public. She admonished us to "act like you had some home training." When I entered the classroom, there were twenty children in the room plus the teacher, who was an older white woman named Mrs. Smith. She looked like someone's grandmother. She was very kind and sweet.

The number of students in the class was far smaller than I had in my first- or second-grade class at Roosevelt. Mrs. Smith introduced me to the class and admonished them to make me feel welcome. Many of the students followed her direction by coming up to me and shaking my hand. One little girl named Paula Baker came over to me, introduced herself, and was very kind and seemed happy to see me. Her skin was very light and fair, but not as light as the other children in the class, and she had extremely long, wavy hair. Over the next few days we became friends. But her race did perplex me. I knew she wasn't white but she didn't look like any Black person that my young seven-year-old eyes had ever seen. I thought she must be a Native American, and I knew that those people had been discriminated against like mine, so I felt comfortable being her friend.

Mamma and Daddy kept asking me if I met the other little Black girl they were told was in my class. They knew her parents and were told that she and her sisters were attending school there. Already thinking my folks were crazy, I kept telling them there wasn't another Black person in my class. This went on for a while, and that made me more curious about Paula, for she was the only person in our class who fit that description. She never talked about a teepee or living on a reservation, or anything else that I associated with Native Americans.

One day I came out and asked her what race she was. She looked me square in the face, put her hands on her hips, and said indignantly, "I am Black, just like you!" Well she put me in my place. That was the end of that discussion. It was never broached again until many years later after we were grown, and she told me she was biracial, which explained her fair features. Finally, I was able to tell Mamma and Daddy that, yes, I had met the other Black girl in my class and that we were friends and I liked her very much.

I stayed at the Advent Episcopal Day School until I graduated from the eighth grade, which was the highest grade Advent hosted. A lot happened during those years. In 1973 Daddy was elected to the Alabama state legislature. He was the first Black person to be elected from our county. As if our family were not already in the spotlight, that made it shine brighter. It was a moment to be proud of. He was elected by Black and white folks together. What made his election unique is that his district was not predominately Black. The city of Midfield was in his district. It was all white and was the last place in the county, according to Mamma, to take the "White Only" and "Colored Only" signs down. But Daddy was amazing with all people. He really charmed those folks and they came out and voted for him.

In 1977 the first of the men who planned and carried out your murder was brought to trial. Robert Chambliss was his name. His nickname was "Dynamite Bob," because he was suspected of causing many of the bombings in Birmingham. What an awful nickname! But I bet he was proud of it. I remember that time very vividly. As you can imagine there was much discussion about it on the TV, radio news, and among friends and family members. It had been fourteen years since your murder, and this was the first time anyone had been tried in court for it. A white man being brought to trial for killing Black people, even in 1977, was huge. I remember I really wanted to see this man and go to the trial. Daddy and Mamma would not let me go to the trial. They said I had to go to school. The officials at Advent must have talked about my safety and Kim's safety during the trial because I recall security for both of us being very tight during that time. I remember that we had to exit the school from an area other than the one used by the other students. Normally all the students sat outside on the sidewalk and waited for our rides to pick us up. Instead, we were picked up out back behind the school and had to stay inside until we were escorted out. It was a little scary.

Daddy didn't even think it was a good idea for Mamma to attend the trial. He did attend, though, and he had to testify. They asked him to identify you by looking at your morgue photos. I can't imagine how painful that must have been. I learned about that part years later.

The closing arguments of the trial took place on what would have been your twenty-sixth birthday. I later learned that Bill Baxley, the prosecutor and attorney general of the state at the time, mentioned it was your birthday in his closing arguments. He stated that there might have been a birthday party at our home—maybe even with grandchildren—if you had lived. It was not long after that that the jury came back with the verdict of guilty for Bob Chambliss and he was given life in prison. I recall being very happy and excited. I did wonder, however, why it had taken fourteen years to convict him. I also later learned that there were four other people who had been identified as participating in planting the bomb, but it would be decades before they were brought to trial and two of them passed away before they were brought to justice.

Chambliss never admitted his guilt. Sadly, none of them did. You would think folks who claimed to be such good "Christians" would try to make amends for the wrongs they have done as our Lord mandates that we do. He did write us a very long letter explaining how he didn't murder you and the other girls and even asked our parents to do what they could to help get him out of jail. Can you believe that? How insulting. People can do some crazy things. That took a lot of nerve.

All of my years at Advent were great. To this day, it was the best seven-year stretch of my life. The Black kids at Advent were sheltered from the outside world, including its problems and its prejudices. We were given much love and attention. What's more, I also received the best education money could buy. We learned things there that took us all the way through college and beyond. I was exposed to things in elementary school that most of my friends from our neighborhood and church didn't learn until they were in their high school and college years.

I would often see my old friend Wendy. We would meet and talk about school and what we were learning. She was shocked that in the third grade I had to write a term paper. Advent was an excellent place to spend my formative years. I never thought on my first day that I would end up having such a great experience, and I think fondly about my time there to this day. The fear I had of the white students and teachers was the exact opposite of what I experienced. Kim and I were always treated with the utmost love, care, and respect. I grew to love everyone in my Advent School family.

I did encounter one young white boy who wasn't fond of me during that first year. I don't recall now whether he disliked all Black folks or just me, but one day he approached me and stated that he was going to fight me when it was time to go out on the playground. This was the moment that I had dreaded from day one, but I had made a vow to myself not to go down without a fight if anyone tried to harm me.

Fighting was not the way I was brought up. We had been trained by those who led the Civil Rights Movement that nonviolence was the way to behave when encountering conflict. It was also the era where people talked of making love, not war, and coming together peacefully. As a kid, I never wanted to harm anyone. I also knew if I got into a fight, there was going to be hell to pay when I got home. Fighting would fall into the category of things for which I could get a whooping. Mamma didn't play about that. She insisted we act like ladies at all times. I knew I couldn't get out of this fight, however, so I was just hoping I could handle myself. We met outside and had a brief discussion, he hit me, and then I popped him a good one. He cried and ran away and I didn't have any more trouble from him. I felt bad about hitting him but I was glad he knew to leave me alone. I wish I had been that brave with Harriett at Roosevelt Elementary.

By the third grade, I found that I was not afraid of bullies and hated injustice of any kind, racial or otherwise, even at that young age. It seemed wrong to me and really made me angry. Even now I really hate it when people are mean to one another for no reason. It is unacceptable to me.

There was a bully in my class by the name of Larry. He was taller than the rest of us and he seemed to always feel the need to push the other students around. For some reason he didn't scare me, but I just couldn't figure him out. I remembered the bullying I got from Harriett at Roosevelt Elementary and I vowed that would never happen again. I was not brave at Roosevelt Elementary and I was ashamed of how I had behaved there. Larry never bothered me; I think it was because his mother liked me.

His mom was a room mother; this was a mother who would come and help the teachers out when we would go on field trips outside of the school or had special activities at the school. Whenever we had parties or field trips, she always came and brought potato chips with some of the best onion dip I had ever tasted. I would sit right near her and eat that dip and tell her how great it was. I thought she made that dip. I learned many years later you could buy it in the grocery store. That didn't matter. It was still DELICIOUS. Maybe she told him to leave me alone.

There was a short guy in our class named Paul whom Larry always picked on. I don't know why he hated that little boy so much and it seemed wrong for him to pick on him so unmercifully.

Crazy me, I always stood up for Paul. I would stand right in front of Larry when he was about to hit Paul and make him stop. I don't know what I was thinking, because I was a short little girl. Paul was the same height as I was, if that. Larry was almost a foot taller than both of us. Also, I was a Black girl breaking up fights between two white boys who didn't have a thing to do with me. I truly had gotten over any fear I had of Advent and the people there by that time. Larry would usually leave Paul alone when I stood up to him. I guess it wasn't as much fun to pick on him when I was around.

I feel bad sometimes that you never got the chance to do what we did by going to Advent. I wonder what your school experience was like, but I guess I will never know. I wonder if you would have been able to adjust to the culture change if you had to attend a predominately white school. I wish more Black kids could have gone to Advent. It was a wonderful educational experience. I certainly wish my Advent experience could have carried on through high school, but unfortunately it did not. A later letter will tell you about my transition to high school, which was a nightmare, but we must learn from even the bad times in life. I miss you lots.

Love,
Lisa

Church Life

Dear Denise,

It's funny I haven't talked about church life. I have some really good and some really painful church memories. Mamma continued to attend 16th Street Baptist Church after your death. Kim and I attended with her after we were born. We were both baptized there. As you know, Daddy was never a member of 16th Street. Kim and I would visit with Daddy at his church, St. Paul Lutheran, from time to time, and I was blessed there as a baby, but we never joined. Uncle Harold and his family joined St. Paul along with Daddy. We all went somewhere different, all Christians but with divergent styles of worship.

Birmingham remains forever altered by what happened to you that September morning. Today, 16th Street Baptist is still in existence as a church but now it is a national historic landmark and part of the National Park Service. The physical structure has gone through a great many changes. They have totally remodeled the basement and made it into an exhibit space telling the history of the whole church. It was very well done. There are memorials to you and the other girls throughout the church. Also, across the street from the church are beautiful statues of you and the other girls. They were erected at the fiftieth anniversary of the bombing. Across the street, too, is the award-winning Birmingham Civil Rights Institute that tells the story of your death, along with other important local events and national events from the Civil Rights Movement. People come from all over the world to learn about what it was like for you when you were growing up, and of course they all learn about what happened to you, Addie Mae, Carole, and Cynthia. Many people also don't know about Sarah Collins Rudolph. She is Addie Mae's sister, and she was also in the bathroom with you all on the day of the bombing. There were five girls in there that day, not four. She was far enough away from you and the others that she was not killed, but she was badly injured and lost an eye. She said the last thing she saw as she turned to look at you all was you asking her sister to tie the sash on your dress. She was the last living person to see you alive. That is very moving for me, and I feel close to her because of that.

I often speak to groups who come through Birmingham to learn more about the Civil Rights Movement. I wish I could talk to you to get your perspective and hear what you remember. You must have heard Reverend Shuttlesworth or Reverend James Bevel, and I bet you also heard Dr. Martin Luther King Jr.—or at least saw them on television or heard them on the radio. Dr. King was killed five years after your death. He was assassinated in Memphis, Tennessee, fighting for the rights of garbage workers. The 1960s were a tough time for our people, but the decades before you were killed were even tougher.

I am grateful that our family carried on after your death to serve the community. As I told you earlier, the name McNair means something here, not only because of your death but also because Daddy was a public servant in politics. He went on to make some controversial headlines later in life, but mostly he was a well-respected politician; maybe we'll talk about that later. For now, let's get back to talking about church.

When I stop to reflect, it's interesting that my church background is just as diverse as the rest of my life has been. I was brought up Baptist, Lutheran, and Episcopalian. Mamma is a Baptist and Daddy is a member of the Lutheran Church, while Kim and I attended an Episcopalian private school. I love that about my upbringing, and consider it a blessing to have experienced my faith in so many different ways.

But I didn't like the fact that Mamma and Daddy didn't worship together. I think worshipping together is important for a couple and their marriage. Also, Kim and I had to choose with whom we were going to go to church each Sunday. Whichever we chose, one parent was going to be disappointed, and you felt it all day, especially if we didn't choose to go with Daddy. He could be quite sensitive about stuff like that, and would have a hurt look on his face all day. Therefore, we knew we had to go with him the following Sunday. Did you have to go through that too? I guess you did.

Later in life, I began to wonder if Dad was disappointed when we joined 16th Street Baptist. After all, it was the church where you were killed, although that certainly wasn't the church's fault. Maybe every time he saw us go off with Mamma, he wondered if we would ever come back. I'm not sure, but he never shared much about his feelings or what he was thinking, which left us guessing.

Mamma was a faithful member of 16th Street Baptist Church, which was one of the the oldest and largest Black churches in the state. It was designed by a famous Black architect named Wallace Rayfield. It is a large church structure, and I later learned that many of the meetings for the Civil Rights Movement were held there, especially the mass meetings leading up to the protests in May 1963. At these meetings they sang songs and received encouragement to carry on. They also were given instructions on how to protest in a nonviolent way. That is why the church was targeted to be bombed. The church is across the street from historic Kelly Ingram Park, where many of the Civil Rights marches of the 1960s started. When I was little, I didn't know any of that history, just that it was Mamma's church. There were many other kids at 16th Street, and most of Mamma's family attended church there. Kim and I enjoyed going there.

I always had a good time when I went to church with Mamma, even though in the back of my mind I understood that you were killed there. There were Sundays when I thought about that a lot; then other times, it never crossed my mind. I remember the bathroom being a creepy place for me because you were killed in the ladies' lounge. By the time I came along, they had remodeled the church and the lounge wasn't even in the same location as it was on the morning you were killed. I still wanted to get in and get out quickly whenever I had to use it.

One Sunday, I was washing my hands at the sink and the water sputtered out with a loud pop as pipes do when the water has been turned off for a bit. It scared me half to death. I don't know how that happened, but I remember screaming and Mamma trying to calm me down.

Like most Black Baptist churches of the era, 16th Street had an all-Black congregation and a Black minister. Some of the people were first-generation professionals, like doctors, lawyers, businessmen, and educators. This was a source of pride for us as Black folks because the opportunity for us to have these types of jobs had not always existed. It gave some of those folks a big head, but most of them were properly proud and they passed that on to us kids in a good way. I was never asked, "Are you going to college?" but "Where are you going to college?"

Our minds were always nurtured, and learning was a must. The church insisted that we do everything with excellence. We were taught to sit up straight and to enunciate properly (which was another reason why I was confused when people told me I talked "white" because I thought I spoke proper English). We rehearsed for Christmas and Easter speeches for weeks at a time. I enjoyed the Christmas and Easter programs, but I was glad when they were over because they were a lot of work. Mamma always made us practice our speeches aloud, making us enunciate, project our voice, and look at the audience as well as memorize speeches.

Daddy's church was different, as I'm sure you saw. It was on the opposite side of town and was a small church compared to 16th Street Baptist. Mamma's church was lively and spirited, but St. Paul Lutheran had a more solemn form of worship, similar to a Catholic or Episcopal church. There were many readings and chants during the liturgy. The one thing that stood out for me the most was my father's congregation was all Black but the pastor and his wife were white. That was definitely not the tradition in the South at that time. Another interesting thing about Daddy's church is that they had the Holy Communion service every Sunday. We only had it on the first Sunday. St. Paul also had real wine—no grape juice for them.

The pastor was Joseph Ellwanger, a tall man whose face and head reminded me of pictures of a much slimmer Benjamin Franklin. I always thought it was odd for a white man to be in a church in a Black neighborhood with the temperament of the times. I have to say, however, that Pastor Ellwanger is one of the nicest men you will ever want to meet. We visited his home often and he and his wife visited ours along with their children. I learned later that they were part of the Civil Rights

Mamma and Daddy with me at my blessing at St. Paul Lutheran Church. From the right to the left; Mamma, me, Daddy, Pastor Ellwanger, Grandmother McNair, Joyce Ellwanger, and Joseph Bowman. Photo from the Chris McNair Archives.

Movement, and were quite active. Today, they are still activists for the cause of justice and are still very dear friends of ours.

Going to church with Daddy was a good experience. The people were nice, and I was proud that the congregation and their white pastor got along so well. I suppose that was my first experience of seeing Black and white people living in harmony outside of school. I figured we didn't have a choice at school but the adults at St. Paul had chosen to be together. Pastor Ellwanger and his wife moved to another church up North and were replaced with another white couple who had lots of kids with whom we got to play.

As the years went by, Daddy went to church less and less and we went to church with Mamma more and more. Kim and I joined 16th Street, but always had fond memories of St. Paul. Daddy said once that he liked what 16th Street did for us and how it nurtured us. That made me feel a little better about not ending up with him at his church.

I'm going to close here and pick up talking about church again later. You will be very surprised at where I attend church now and how I got there. But that can wait; I still have to tell you about some other adjustments and personal growth experiences I had on my way to being who I am today.

Much love,
Lisa

Thinking White

Dear Denise,

I didn't spend much time with the kids from my neighborhood once I began attending Advent Episcopal Day School. Advent was downtown and about twenty minutes from home. Daddy had to drive us there every morning because school buses didn't take us to Advent. After school, Daddy would pick us up and, instead of going straight home, we went to his place of business. He was a professional photographer and had his own studio in town. He started that business in 1962, when you were still alive.

It was easier for us to go there after school because it was near downtown. After 5 p.m., either Daddy or his assistant would take us home. By the time we got home, it was time to do more homework, eat dinner, and then go to bed. We rarely saw the kids in the neighborhood except for weekends and school breaks.

I didn't have as many friends in the neighborhood as our sister, Kim. There were many children her age to play with, but there were only two girls my age. One was shy and didn't come out of her house much; the other one had a father who was a bishop with the Church of God in Christ and he traveled a lot. When I was at home and not working to complete the mountain of homework we got from Advent, I loved to go outside and play with my dogs in our back yard, read the encyclopedia, or watch TV. I loved to watch old black-and-white movies with Mamma. The only person from Roosevelt Elementary School who I really had contact with was my friend Wendy.

I didn't mind telling Wendy about repeating the second grade because I found out she had to repeat a grade also. That drew us even closer together as friends. Wendy lived about seven or eight minutes away, however, so we mostly wrote letters or occasionally talked on the phone. Young kids weren't allowed to talk on the phone very much back then. We only got to see each other when our mothers were able to arrange it.

I have always liked being around people, so making friends and getting along with my teachers was not difficult for me. I made friends with many of the white children in the class. Stacey Bentley was a cute little girl who reminded me of the actress Sandy Duncan, who I saw a lot of on TV. Jane Ackridge was also a close friend of mine, and we were in the same class together for many years. Jane was the person who shared with me where babies really came from. At first, I didn't believe her, because that was not the story that Mamma had told me. I later found out that Mamma had left a great deal out of her account.

Advent had French classes and every student took them until they graduated. I found French fascinating and the teacher said my pronunciation was excellent. When Wendy and I compared what we learned, it was so different. At the time, I only knew we went to different schools, but didn't know why. I didn't learn until much later that my parents paid for us to go to Advent and it was a private school, while Roosevelt was a free public school.

It was years later that I learned the value of a private school education and came to appreciate what a higher level of education it provided. As I mentioned earlier, I distinctly remember having to write my first research paper in the third grade. Many of my public-school friends didn't write a research paper until they were in their junior or senior year of high school, and some not even until they were in college.

The teachers, who were all white, were very good to me. They never treated me any differently from any of the white students. Mamma was surprised and often asked, "Aren't there *any* Black teachers there?" In my last years there, we had one Black substitute teacher. I was thrilled to see someone of color work with excellence at the school I loved, but people of color were clearly in the minority at Advent.

I asked Mamma one time while I was in elementary school if I was supposed to hate white people. I asked because I was at Advent with so few Black people, and I knew some folks in the African American community vehemently hated white folks. I also saw on television some of the bad things happening to Black people at the hands of white racists, and I would think about you. I was trying to figure out if I was supposed to like them or not. I wondered if hatred was the standard way of relating to white people? Yet, all of the folks at Advent were very nice to us. Also, all of Daddy's friends who were white were super nice. It left me very confused.

Mamma said, "We have to love all people like Christ loves us. Everyone has a duty to love and we must take each person individually and love them for who they are." That made sense to me as a child, particularly because it was confusing to me to be in a white school every day with white students, teachers, and friends, along with all the other white friends we had in our life. If I had to hate them, I knew it was going to be difficult and require time and energy that I didn't have.

For years, there were never more than two students in my class who were African Americans, and I was one of them. Spending that much time with people of another race, although quite strange at the beginning, soon became the norm for me. I had been used to a totally African American world, except when I went to a store away from my neighborhood or when I went to church with Daddy.

During those years, something subtle was happening to me but I didn't realize it. Before I knew it, I was more comfortable with things in the "white culture." It happened so gradually that I didn't even notice for a while that my dialect changed drastically, and when I did notice, it was only because family members and friends started to point it out: "You talk like a white girl."

At first, I was confused. After all, wasn't I speaking the English language? As I began to observe and listen to other kids at church with our family members, I did notice the difference. Their English was excellent, but our dialects were definitely different.

Early on at Advent, this difference was not that big of a deal to me. I was a kid living my life. The people I spent the better part of my day with spoke and acted like I did, so what difference did it make? As I grew older, this significant difference began to profoundly affect the way I looked at life and how I distinguished and valued the differences between Black and white folks, not just in the South but all over our country.

More and more, the Black kids I knew outside Advent didn't want much to do with me. I didn't relate to their world or know their slang. I always had to ask them what things meant, like the use of the word "*bad*" for something that was actually good. People thought I was odd to ask why we would call something good *bad*. Although segregation was eventually against the law and we could work, play, attend school together, and socially interact, white folks and Black folks for the most part *did not get along*. We were now able to do things together but we didn't know how to be real friends. We were Southern, so we knew how to be cordial and polite. At the end of the day, however, white people had their lives and we had ours, and rarely did the twain meet. I was breaking all those social mores by functioning in both worlds. Dr. King's dream was alive in my life, and I was playing a part in its fulfillment.

Here is another example of how different I was from the rest of my Black peers. When we rode in the car with Mamma, she always kept the radio on the easy listening station or, on Sundays, the Black gospel music station. When riding with Daddy, we listened to country or classical music, and NPR (National Public

Radio) on long trips. We rarely if ever listened to music the other kids were listening to, like R&B or rock and roll.

I remember distinctly when our first cousins Lynn and Nedric, invited me to go to a Jackson Five concert that was being held here in Birmingham. I really didn't want to go, but Mamma thought it would be good for me, so I went. I didn't want to hear that loud rock music from those "Black people." The Jackson Five were popular then, but not with me. Michael Jackson eventually went mainstream (white people loved him) and became a huge crossover artist. For the most part, white folks had their music and we had ours, and I didn't know too many people who listened to both. By the way, the concert was exciting and interesting, and I had a very good time.

That "evil Rock and Roll," as I called it, was not so bad and, like many young girls of the time, I fell madly in love with Michael Jackson. I swore that when I grew up, I was going to marry him. The concert experience reinforced in my thinking that my life was miles apart from my cousins who lived in Birmingham and with whom I spent a good amount of time. They were Black and cool and knew all things Black that I didn't—and they did it so effortlessly. They went to public school with only Black kids, and they also socialized and hung out with all Black kids. Although they were intelligent, they had a sense of self that connected them with our race that I didn't realize I was gradually losing—if I ever had it. It is so difficult to admit that I had trouble being something that should have come naturally for me. I carried a great deal of shame about this for many years.

Daddy was a state representative in the Alabama legislature for part of the time when Kim and I were at Advent. We often heard talk at home about politics and the state of African American life in America. We had a good life because of Daddy's political position. People treated us with an extra bit of kindness because of your murder, but also tended to treat us like celebrities because of Daddy's position in politics.

Many white folks felt guilty that their hate or their predecessors' hate led to your death and the deaths of the three other girls killed with you. The way Daddy and Mamma handled themselves after the bombing also earned them the respect of even some of the most hateful racists. Our parents did not espouse hate, but modeled forgiveness and bucked the status quo to create a life for us in this city. I am proud of them for that, and I'm sure you would be too.

Our way of life, however, gave me a false sense of how things were for other Black folks in Birmingham and throughout the entire country, but especially in the South. Going to school with upper- and middle-class white and Black kids gave me the sense that everything for Black people was a-okay. When I saw Black folks on TV complain about racism and how they were mistreated, I found it annoying, and would think, "Why are those people complaining? What is wrong with them? Things are good. They must not be working hard enough." Often, when I heard of someone not getting a job or being arrested and claiming they had been treated unfairly due to the color of their skin, I would get irritated and wish they would shut up.

What I didn't understand was that my thinking echoed that of the people with whom I spent most of my time, the folks at school—white people. They couldn't relate to the average Black person and, eventually, neither could I. One critical difference between those white folks and me was that I was *always* going to be Black, and white people, other than the ones I attended school with, would look at me like they looked at all other Black people.

Although I knew how wonderful my life was, when I walked out of my door I was just another nigger, just another disgruntled Black person in the eyes of most white people at that time. I didn't realize that talking down to and negatively portraying my own people was not helping us as a race; but more important for me, my attitude created a distaste in me for my own people which in the long run was going to do me more harm than good. It would harm not only me, but the race as a whole. Not only that, but it gave me an inflated positive estimation of what I thought of white folks and all things white. I too began to think all things white were better than things Black, which was very sad because the Black people around me were awesome and just as wonderful as the white people around me— probably even more so because of all of the obstacles in their ways.

I wonder what you would have thought of me when I started doing this? I often wonder if you would have been able to understand me and why I thought as I did. It would have been nice to have a big sister to share things with. You would have been more grounded in what it was like growing up Black in the South, and perhaps could have helped me keep a proper perspective. My sheltered school life meant that I had lots of adjustments to make before I finally learned to be comfortable with my characteristics from both worlds in which I lived—the Black and the white.

Love,
Lisa

High School Was Painful

Dear Denise,

Advent was such an amazing experience. It was hard to replicate. When it came time to decide what high school to go to, I had a number of options to choose from. Daddy wanted me to attend another predominately white private school called Altamont. I took the entrance exam to attend, passed with flying colors, and received a full scholarship. I got to take a tour of the school and it was fantastic. It had the latest of everthing. Even lunch was going to be stellar, as they served each table family style. Yum!!! But I knew I didn't want to go to another all-white private school. I told Daddy this and he was less than pleased. If I had attended Altamont, at the time I would have been one of only three Black kids in the entire school. This would have taken me further from Black culture and totally eliminated my chance of dating in high school. I wanted to date, and I knew that white guys would not date me because I was Black.

That being said, I also wanted to go to a good school. There was a very good Catholic school in town with a large number of Black students, and I knew many people who had attended there. There was also Ramsay High, a magnet school that was a part of the Birmingham public school system. Paula went there and I knew if she liked it I would too. I was also interested in art and there was an art high school called the Alabama School of Fine Arts, ASFA for short. I was good in the visual arts and that was one of the specialties that they offered. I thought it might be a lot like Advent and its student population was much more diverse. It was also downtown. You had to take a test there too and see what your skills were in your chosen art. I did, and I got in. It also didn't cost nearly as much as Advent, just a small monthly stipend. This way I would be able to help Mamma and Daddy save money. I was really looking forward to starting high school at ASFA. Sadly, it was just a little too much of a culture shock: leaving the comfort of Advent as well as the usual adjustments to high school. Artistic children are very different, and it wasn't a good fit. I also struggled with my homework and made some of the first bad grades in my life. Up until that time I had been an A and B honor roll student.

I finished my freshman year at ASFA. I was really not looking forward to going back for another year, but I never said anything about it to Mamma and Daddy. I was already feeling bad about not choosing to go where Daddy really wanted to me to go; he had researched ASFA and was satisfied with me attending school there. I wasn't sure what he would say if I told him I was not pleased with this school either. I thought that maybe I should go to a nearby public school where our neighbors all went. Sadly, I never got the nerve to tell either one of them until the morning of my sophomore year of high school. I was getting dressed and pressing my clothes for the day, and I had a complete come-apart. I began crying and pleading with Mamma not to make me go back to that school. She didn't know what to make of my behavior. I was always the levelheaded child who never made waves and was always very obedient. It wasn't like me to fly off the handle, but this morning was different. I just kept saying, "I can't go back!!! Please don't make me go back!" I am sure Mamma thought something horrible had happened. She went to tell Daddy and I could hear her saying, "I don't know, she just keeps saying, 'don't make me go back.'" Once I calmed down, they asked me what I wanted to do. So later that morning they enrolled me in Midfield High School. Unfortunately, I was several days behind because they had started school already. It was weird, but at least I didn't have to go back to ASFA.

Despite my feelings, ASFA was a great school and I did have some good memories there. I loved the art I got to do. One of my favorite experiences was the day we went to do charcoal drawings in a cemetery. At first I thought the teacher had to be kidding: draw in a cemetery? But it turned out to be a very cool experience. Headstones are amazing and beautiful. There is so much history in a cemetery. Each headstone represents a life. I am still fascinated with cemeteries and really like walking around them reading the headstones.

Midfield was such a different experience from Advent or ASFA, and I never stopped looking for what I had experienced at Advent. What's more, at a time when I needed some help understanding who I was and what was going on around me, I found none of that at Midfield.

The issue of race didn't come up often when I was at Advent. Either the kids didn't exhibit any racist attitudes toward me or they were simply being polite. I found Midfield to be quite polarized when it came to race. Midfield was a public school near where I lived. It was made up of approximately 65 percent white students and 35 percent Black students. The teachers and administrators were mostly white. I remember there being only five Black teachers. But the racial pressure was really heavy for the Black students and teachers. They were nice and kind but they were afraid, too. If there was an incident, you really could not count on them to have your back. They were in danger of losing their jobs if they said something. That was really not very comforting. I didn't know then that the Black students had been bused there, and neither student group was happy about it. The Black students missed their school and resented the fact that they had no say in how things went there. The white students simply didn't want Black students there, period. On my first day there, I could tell that the white and Black students did not get along. Some of the Black kids told me that there were some white students who were members of the Ku Klux Klan attending school there and, if I asked, they would show me their membership card. I was thinking right then that I might have made a mistake deciding to go there, and I wanted to change my mind—again.

I didn't know many of the Black kids who went there. If you remember, I left public school in second grade because I wasn't getting a good education, and when I first went to Advent they made me repeat the second grade, despite Daddy's objections. I was glad they did that because I knew that I had not learned anything at Roosevelt in the second grade. If I realized that and I was only a second grader, you know it must have been bad.

I started Midfield in the tenth grade and, as I explained, a few days late because their school had already begun. All the boys I knew from my neighborhood were in the eleventh grade, and that made it even more difficult to connect with the few people I did know. I wanted friends desperately.

In time, I did make friends, some white and others Black. One of my Black friends was a twin named Sonya. She was nice, but she was kind of quiet, shy, and bookish, and was in the band. I tried extending myself to her, but the group she hung with wasn't overly welcoming and tended to have their own cliques. They knew each other better because they had been going to school together for their entire lives. I was the new kid on the block. I tried calling her at home, after school, but she didn't reach out to me nearly as much. In all fairness, it's hard to come into a school with folks who have been together since elementary school. I was new and very different from anyone they knew. As you can see, the memories are still painful for me to recall.

Not long after I enrolled, everyone figured out that you, my sister, were one of the girls who had been killed in the church bombing, and that Daddy was a public official. For some reason, that made everyone think I was rich because I came from a famous family. Most of the students at Midfield were from blue-collar families who saw us as people of privilege. That assumption, which I have encountered a lot, is one thing that has always irritated me.

Just because we were famous didn't mean we were rich. It still doesn't. Quite the contrary, if people knew the real truth about it. The two things do *not* go hand in hand, and I was constantly trying to get folks to understand that. I argued that the poor hungry kids on the CARE charity commercials were famous, but not rich. I just wanted to be treated like a regular kid, not a celebrity.

I also wanted to connect more with other African Americans. Even then I felt that I had missed something in that part of my upbringing. I felt odd and didn't fit in with my own people most of the time. As far as dating was concerned, none of the white guys were going to ask me out. It didn't happen at Advent and

The student council during my senior year of high school. I was the president of the council. I am on the front row, second from the right. Courtesy of the author.

it sure wasn't going to happen at blue-collar Midfield. That type of interracial dating rarely occurred in Alabama. It was still very taboo. A white guy would be your friend, but would never openly date you.

There was one bright spot during my time at Midfield, and it was a life-changing experience. I found that I enjoyed being part of the student council, and I was a good class representative. I had been involved in the student council at Advent, and maybe some of Daddy's politics rubbed off on me! I was part of the student council all three years I was at Midfield. Then, at the end of my junior year, it came time to elect officers for our student council. In any other organization, I had been part of, I had always held an office and most of the time it was either president or vice president. Therefore, I decided that I wanted to be student government president. I declared my candidacy, and my opponent was a white student.

There was only one other Black person who had won that position at Midfield High School, and his name was Theo Lawson. His mother and our Mamma were in the same sorority and had been friends for years. He was a friend of the family and I had known him during his senior year at Midfield. I thought I could do it, and I wanted to do it. I ran, and it was a fascinating experience.

The African Americans at school, for the most part, had no hope; they acted as if they had no future. It was sad to see our people without hope, doubting that anything good would ever happen to them. The African Americans in my church and social circle didn't look at life like that at all. For the most part, the Midfield students didn't ask which college they were going to. Their thinking was more along the lines of, "Boy, I can't wait to graduate. I wonder what I will do then?" Or they would say things like, "I will be really glad to get out of this place," as if it were a prison. That was true for most of the Black students and many of the white ones, too.

They didn't think about college, only about getting a job—and some didn't even think about that. So, it was tough for me to relate to them because that wasn't my reality. Most of the Black students at Midfield were apathetic and it would show up in their behavior in small ways. For example, they would almost never cheer at pep rallies for the football games and had little if any school spirit. I would always cheer and a lot of times I was the only person of color who did, other than the students in the band. That made me stand out even more and feel very much alone. Actually, alone is not the right term, I felt more like a weirdo, like someone who was really out of place. Also, because many of the students were bused in, they didn't want to be there, and the white teachers and students really didn't make them feel welcome and didn't want them there either.

I understand that this was a problem for many of our people. Segregation had created pockets of hopelessness in the hearts and minds of many of our Black citizens. They were simply thinking about existence, and that was how it had been for their parents and their parents before them. To break out of that hopelessness took a lot of support and courage, and many of their parents were downtrodden and discouraged. They could not help their children because there was no one to help them or lift them up. This was their life in the South and in Alabama. This was a sad sight to see. I had never experienced anything like it—such complete and utter hopelessness. High school was such a depressing time.

When I ran for student council president, many of the Black students didn't understand why I would even attempt to do that, since the school was 65 percent white. One of the Black girls I met on my first day at Midfield was named Mary Jordan. She was in my homeroom throughout my time there. Her nickname was "Pig," for some reason. I told her I wasn't going to call her Pig, because her mother gave her the beautiful name of Mary Frances and she was not a pig.

We weren't fast friends because she already had her own circle of friends, but she was nice to me; she would talk to me and tell me things to help me get by. She made me feel like I was a part of the school. When I wanted to know what was really going on, Mary would tell me the real deal. She came and reported to me what most of the students felt about my candidacy. Mary told me that she hoped I would win and was going to vote for me. She went on to say, however, that "they," meaning the white students, weren't going to *let* me win. "Let," as if they had some sort of total control of the matter. I told her that I could win if everyone who was Black voted for me, and that I had a feeling a lot of white students were going to vote for me also. Despite the racial tension at Midfield I had made a number of white friends. I worked hard and got my name out there as best I knew how.

On the day of the election I was very nervous. I felt I had a great chance to win but this was still the South, and this was Midfield, and racisim is real. When the votes were counted they announced the election results over the PA system. I was declared the winner by a very large margin! It was my best day at Midfield High School. The Black kids jumped up and down, and they were jubilant. The white kids were happy for me too, and many would high-five me in the hallway.

I went and talked to my opponent and wished her well. Mary came to me with tears in her eyes and congratulated me for winning the election, but I corrected her that *we* had done it together. A group of white guys—I guess you would say they were the cool guys of the school—were really nice to me. That whole next year when I would see them in the hallway, they would shout "Prez!" For the first time, I had fun in school and people liked me! It was a victory for me, but more so for the African American population at our school. I like to think I gave them hope and something to be proud of. I think they even walked a little taller. That was the one good thing I remember from Midfield.

My year as president was a good year. I learned a lot about being a good leader. One skill that I learned was to delegate responsibility and not try to do all the work myself. I had a good rapport with the students as well as the faculty. I thought things were going to be okay, but I was being too optimistic.

As president, I could have assemblies and bring in special speakers, but had to coordinate and work with the faculty. Naturally, I wanted to celebrate Black History Month. I thought it would be good to share the accomplishments of African Americans with my fellow students. The powers that be gave their approval but when it came time to actually celebrate, they blocked me at every turn, and finally I was told not to focus on Black History Month any further. They didn't mind me having a speaker, just not one who celebrated Black History Month. They broke my heart by telling me no, but also by dancing around it instead of just saying they didn't want to have that type of program at their school.

It reminds me of the debate we are having now in America. All across the country, schools are banning a concept they are calling "Critical Race Theory." The bans are vague, but they are basically saying they don't want our history taught because it might make white kids feel bad. It reminds me so much of how I was treated my senior year at Midfield. The truth is they don't want our story told, they don't want Civil Rights history told, they don't want the truth told about how this country has treated African Americans—not for just a year or two, not for only a decade, but for centuries. What they don't want are white kids to really know the truth, because if they did our country would be very different. It has been surpressed for years. They have just now given a name to it and are making laws about it to scare teachers from teaching true history . . . our shared American history. But we have the Internet now. They can't hide it forever because they can't shut that down.

It really breaks my heart. In the past few years I have talked with many of my white friends about the Civil Rights Movement. They have come to me, and so many of them don't know what most Black folks know about our history. These folks are sixty and seventy years old. The surpression of this knowledge is real and deliberate. They know if peole know what really happened they would change things going forward because if we know our history, we will hopefully not repeat it. Decent people really need to stand up for this to stop, just like they needed to stand up back in 1963. Like Mamma always says, "right is right and right don't wrong nobody."

A few years after I graduated, one of my neighbors, a smart African American young lady, was also elected to be the student council president, and we both hoped that things had changed. Sadly, she too was not allowed to celebrate Black History Month with a speaker or a program. They just didn't want anything positive about our race and our people to be shown. A program like that would have lifted the students up, both Black and white. I even went to bat for her to try to see if I could get the school to change their minds. A local disc jockey who was very well liked and well known had a child at that school. I thought his influence would help me change the minds of the establishment. He was afraid and refused to help me. It was sad to learn that white people still had so much power over us and that so many of our people were afraid of them. This was 1983, almost twenty years after your death. It was during times like these when I would ask myself, "why do I live in this state, and why haven't I left?" At the time of this letter it is 2021, and I am asking myself the same question. God must have me here for a reason.

I told you that the Black students seemed downcast and defeated all the time, and it made sense based on all of the things that had happened to our people over the years in Alabama and in America. That makes what Mamma and Daddy did after your death all the more remarkable. They refused to live with the status quo, but set out to make a new life for Kim and me and for all the other people with whom they worked and lived. Our people have had to learn to live with pain and carry on with life. I lived with some pain and I carried on. Years later I would meet up again with Mary, who so kindly supported my run for president. I will share that with you later.

Love,
Lisa

LETTER 12

Buried Pain Will Come Up Again

Dear Denise,

A few years ago, I was invited back to Midfield to give a speech at a teacher's workshop before the start of the school year. All the teachers and administrators from the high school and the school district were expected to attend. I had not dealt with how painful that whole high school experience had been, and had not really given it much thought. Instead, I had moved on and didn't process it. It was high school and that was long done and gone, or so I thought.

The morning I was to go to Midfield for my speech, my spirit was heavy and I felt nothing but dread and sorrow while I was getting ready, similar to the feeling I had when I did not want to return to the Alabama School of Fine Arts for my sophomore year. I like speaking in public and had done quite a bit of it all that year, so I knew that was not the reason for my anxiety. My speech was ready, but I was not. As I was driving up to the school, I realized I had only been back twice since graduation, and one of those times was when Kim graduated.

I started to feel like crying. I don't like people to see me cry. I prefer to tough it out and do my crying in private, in my car mostly. I was getting out of the car, making sure I had all my stuff, and fighting to hold back the tears. I tried to pull myself together. "This was ridiculous," I thought. "Why in the world was I crying?" But to no avail. I prayed and asked God to help me keep my composure. I was thinking, "Why do I feel this way? All that stuff was such a long time ago."

I walked into the cafeteria where everyone had gathered for breakfast before the program. I found the lady who had invited me, and she greeted me and gave me my instructions for the day. She was talking, but the whole time I was desperately trying not to break down. I had a big lump in my throat and couldn't eat a thing. I started to cry, just a little at first but then full-blown, uncontrollable tears.

Through my sobs, I explained to the lady who invited me that I didn't know it would hurt so much to come back and that I had ignored the residue of all the fear, sadness, and meanness I had felt almost every day I attended school there. She patted me on the back, and kindly let me have my moment alone. I went off and cried for almost thirty minutes. I guess that I had been hurt at Midfield more than I thought I had, and just being back there opened the floodgates of tears and pain. It makes me think about the pain we all feel as Black people in this country. It has been so much and gone on for so long we just become accustomed to it. But ultimately we are probably walking around with undiagnosed PTSD (that means Post Traumatic Stress Disorder). That is definitely what I had that day, a PTSD episode.

I spoke to the group and it went well. Today, Midfield is totally different than when I was there. It is made up of ninety percent Black students and most of the faculty is Black as well. The principal I met that day was Black too. I recounted my story about becoming student body president. I told them about Mary and how I refused to call her Pig. Just then, a woman in the back of the auditorium yelled something, and I looked up and saw Mary standing there, waving to me. That was it. I lost it, and while I cried, Mary cried and then many in the audience were crying. I finished our story as Mary came down and gave me a big hug. She now works in the cafeteria at Midfield, and has a child who graduated from there. God does work in mysterious ways.

After attending Midfield, I had a greater appreciation for people who are in the generation before me. They went on to live their lives but had to carry so much sorrow, unresolved grief, and hurt. I have already explained that after your death, all students just went back to school on the following Monday. There was no grief counseling, no time to mourn, no memorials, and no national news reporting live from the scene. Everyone went back to his or her daily lives.

Black folks could not protest or insist on an investigation. Everyone lived in fear that it would happen again, *knew* it could happen again, so they just kept their mouths closed, shoved their pain deeper into the recesses of their hearts, and moved on. Yet in moving on, they were carrying a heavy load of sorrow. They learned to live with it, they learned to mask it, but that did not make it go away. I found that out on the day I returned for my speech at Midfield.

I am now Facebook friends with a lot of my white former classmates and a few of the Black ones too. We even have a private Facebook group to keep in touch. It's interesting how friendly and kind they all have been. I have been to several reunions and have been one of only a handful of African Americans who attended, but I am glad I have gone each time. What I didn't know is the effect I had on the lives of some of my fellow students. Some have reached out to me to let me know that because they knew me in high school they think differently about Black people and racism in this country. I didn't think they even cared. It is very heart-warming to know that I was able to make a difference. Praise the Lord.

I wonder what your high school life and experience would have been like? You would have been so popular and a great friend to everyone, and you would have been my friend, too.

Love ya,
Lisa

More Messed-Up Thinking

Dear Denise,

The mind is such an interesting creation. It can be twisted and manipulated to see and believe all sorts of things, and then what we believe and think sometimes becomes part of our subconscious so completely that we aren't aware of what or how we think. It takes work to change a mind, and my mind needed a lot of changing.

I was always taught to be proud of myself—not in a cocky way, but so I would not think negatively about myself. Many people don't receive that message, and I am thankful for my family encouraging me to take pride in myself; to be proud of ourselves as African Americans in this country and the contributions we brought to this land we love. We were taught not to believe it when white people said that Black people were lazy and no good; rather, that we had worth and value. I know you were taught the same way. Still, other subtler, more negative messages were being directed at me every day. Without realizing it, those messages got into my mind and heart and started to bring me down.

When I was younger, there was a saying and even a song that stated, "Say it loud, I'm Black and I'm proud." We as a race, however, haven't always behaved and lived in a way that showed that we actually believed that. I overheard some of my relatives saying things in reference to our people like, "Well, you know colored people ain't gonna do right," or "What color is your doctor? Black? Well you better get a white doctor. I wouldn't be caught dead going to a Black doctor," or "white businesses give better service."

If there was a Black-owned business and there was another, white-run business that provided the same services, often our people would go to the white one if they could. For some reason, we thought that white was better. Through the years of segregation and Jim Crow all we wanted to have was the same services and opportunities that white folks had, but that seemed to later translate into "What they (white folks) have is better than what we have," even though what we had in our neighborhoods had served us well through all the years of segregation.

This thinking led to the downfall of many Black-owned businesses after integration came about. Once we had the opportunity to go somewhere else, we did, and many of us left the Black community to shop and live in white communities. We were excited to have the opportunity to take part in businesses in a way we had never been allowed to before. This was not a bad thing, but it had a devastating effect on Black businesses. We didn't do it maliciously, and I don't think we could see the harm it did as we lost our Black neighborhood businesses along with their tax revenue for our community. In our effort to have equal opportunities and services, we forgot about the good that we did have.

The standard for beauty when I was young was a woman who was tall, thin, blonde, young, and white. The women who were chosen to be Miss America always fit that description. That's also who we saw regularly portrayed on television and in commercials. That image of a woman was on all the sitcoms and soap operas, on the drama shows and in the movies. I was probably six years old when I saw the first credible Black female character on TV: Diahann Carroll played a widowed nurse trying to raise her young son on a show called *Julia*. You had better not call any Black family on the phone at the time Diahann Carroll's show would come on each week because everyone knew what the others were doing. We almost never got to see many Black people on TV, unless they were entertainers invited by some white guy to his entertainment show. We were rarely depicted in TV shows and most Black entertainers didn't have their own shows—they were featured on someone else's show. The shows that were headlined by Black stars didn't last long.

My first strong Black male figure on TV was Greg Morris on *Mission Impossible*. He was never on the screen for very long, nor did he have very many lines to say, but I was thrilled to see him. Back then there wasn't cable TV like there is now, but I watched a lot of TV, as most kids did. Now that I think about it, *Mission Impossible* was an hour show and *Julia* was a half-hour. Who was on TV the rest of the time? White folks! White folks on the news, white folks on daytime drama, white folks in comedies, white folks in drama. White people were all over the screen, even in all of the commercials.

Now, what did all this do? Unbeknownst to us, many were developing a complex that being white was better because that was what everyone seemed to prefer. On top of that, we had our own personal bias that considered darker-skinned Black folks less desirable than those with lighter skin. Did you ever hear, "If you are light, you are all right"? That thinking hasn't helped our cause at all, and has caused us much confusion and heartache.

My skin tone is what you would call the color of caramel. From looking at your pictures, you were a little lighter. I am not dark brown or black (sometimes called blue-black if someone was really dark; I like to think of that color as black currant, which I think is a beautiful grape), but I'm not light either. The only thing that made me somewhat noticeable was my long hair, which the boys seemed to like. Other than that, it was understood that all the little high-yellow girls (as we called the light-skinned girls) were considered pretty. The rest of us were just "okay."

I already mentioned that in the first grade I became friends with Wendy, who happened to be very light-skinned. She was the most popular girl in the class, maybe even the school. Her father taught at the school and that added to her popularity. Mamma told me to look for her because she knew her mother. Wendy's mother was also a teacher and I believe she and Mamma taught at the same school for a time.

I was used to getting attention and I don't mind telling you that it bothered me as a six-year-old to have to share that attention with Wendy or anyone else. I was an only child and, after your death, everyone was so happy that I was born, which is why I suppose I received a great deal of attention and love. I reasoned that I should hang out with Wendy, and then maybe some of the attention given to her would trickle down to me. It seems so stupid to have thought that way now, but I want to be honest in everything I share with you. She was also a really nice person and still is to this day.

We got along well and have remained life-long friends. From that moment, however, I thought, "Wendy is the cute one and I am just okay," based solely on her skin tone. Truth be told, neither one of us thought of ourselves as raving beauties, and some would categorize us as nice-looking girls. That bias in favor of light skin gave Wendy points with others (especially with the guys) that to this day I don't think she knows she has. That is why we remained friends, because she was and is a truly wonderful person with a big heart who is in no way pretentious. All that silly skin-color nonsense didn't and doesn't mean anything to her. She is a down-to-earth person and I am glad we are still friends.

As our teen years progressed, Wendy and I would hang out as teenagers tend to do. We went to the movies, the mall (I don't think you had those yet when you were alive), and the skating rink. Without fail, boys would come up to her and strike up a conversation. They would come in pairs, and both guys would talk to her. I might as well have been invisible. I often fantasized about what I could have done if I had been light skinned for a week (or even a day) and what difference that would have made or what kind of person I would have become with that opportunity. Would it have made a difference in what kind of person I became? Would it have improved my chances for dating?

The low self-worth of Black folks began to consume my thinking and affect my identity. Even though I thought well of myself, all those images and impressions instilled through the dominant white culture and the twisted way we as Black folks looked at each other weighed me down. What's more, the media constantly reported about Black-on-Black crime in the inner city, depicting us in a bad light and rarely saying anything positive about us or highlighting our achievements.

I was in a private school with middle- and upper-class white students who would say things like, "You're not really Black" or "You're different; you're not like *those people*." But I doubt if they knew any other Black folks. I think they only knew what society said Black people were supposed to be like. Why did their perceptions have to automatically be negative instead of positive? The result was that I actually started to believe I was different. When I would see a Black man dressed in a shabby way, I would grab my purse. I would look the other way and not speak because I thought I had nothing in common with him.

I have already told you that some of these attitudes permeated my outlook so completely that I would sometimes listen to some Black folks talk about how the white man was oppressing or discriminating against our people and think, "What are you complaining about? You must just be lazy; you should get a job. White people are not like that anymore." Of course, that was the world in my mind. White folks discriminated then, and they still do to this day. Not all white people do, but a greater number than I knew. Racism is systemic in the country.

I've come a long way when it comes to confronting my thinking about Black and white issues, and I suppose I have a long way to go. It's tough confronting your own mindsets, especially when that puts you at odds with your family and community. Oh, Denise, it's time to go to bed. There's so much more I want to tell you and I will pick this topic back up in my next letter.

Love,
Lisa

The Year of the Debutante

Dear Denise,

The South still maintains the tradition of "coming-out" events that are also referred to as debutante balls. Parents present young ladies to the community at large as having been suitably trained and groomed for adult life, which of course includes preparation for dating and marriage. Naturally, there was a Black debutante process and a white one in Alabama, as in most other places in the South. They never merged, so no Black debutantes would be at the white version and vice versa. That is true even today.

Mamma was in the inaugural class of debutantes in the Black community here in Birmingham. Therefore, I wanted to be a debutante and she wanted me to be one as well. When I decided to participate, I thought, "Finally, I can be around some peers who had similar backgrounds and experiences." I thought that would make my life like what I had become accustomed to at Advent, which was my ongoing objective after I graduated. My mind was made up: I was going to be a deb. I also hoped I would meet a Black guy to date who had some of the same life experiences that I did. Finding a guy like that would be good because we would have the best of both worlds. The chance of me finding a white guy to like me in Alabama was most likely never ever going to happen. This would kill two birds with one stone.

Well, the whole experience was disappointing and once again less than I had hoped it would be. There were forty-two girls in my debutante class. Most of the girls I had never met before, which was okay, but the girls already had formed a few cliques, and it seemed to me like they had hung out a sign that said, "No new members accepted at this time." All my insecurities came to the forefront, and I had the sense right away that they didn't care for me because I was awkward and not very stylish at all.

What's more, many of them had been acquainted with each other for years through school or their families' social circles. Another thing that made me stand out was where we lived: a good twenty to thirty minutes from the heart of Birmingham. Many of my fellow debutantes-in-training lived near my grandmother

Dear Dear. She lived in Titusville, which was an all-Black neighborhood in the city limits of Birmingham. Most of the homes were new and mostly owned by Black middle-to-upper-class people. They were mostly doctors, lawyers, teachers, and members of other white-collar professions. We were proud of the folks who lived there because they were our best and brightest. This neighborhood was much closer to downtown, church, and everything fun and cool about Birmingham. It wasn't cool to live where we lived. I never liked that we lived so far from town and the people that we spent a great deal of time with, including most of the people who attended 16th Street. It always seemed like we were a half-hour away from anything. So not only did I go to a different school, I lived in an area that not that many people were aware of. It always seemed like we lived on the other side of the world.

I discovered that some of the girls were members of two high school sororities that existed for Black girls in Birmingham, the Marquettes and the Juliets. They were made up of the "in" girls. I had no desire to be part of either club because I knew I would not fit in with them. There was another organization called Jack and Jill. It is international, with chapters all over the world, and made of mostly upwardly mobile African Americans. Birmingham has a chapter, and Mamma got us involved with them. I was enjoying my experience with them. That could have been the piece of the puzzle I was looking for. Well, that didn't last long. Daddy thought they were uppity and told Mamma to take us out of that club. I was really sad. What he didn't know was that I really needed to be a part of a group like that to give balance to my life, especially where my Blackness was concerned. I soon concluded that my preparations for the debutante ball would be yet another sad and lonely experience, but I went through with it anyway because I am not a quitter and it made Mamma happy.

I had bought into the belief that being a debutante meant that we as young ladies were coming out to society for the first time, eligible to have first dates. Boy, was I naive. Not only had many of these girls been dating for years, they had been doing a lot more than that, if you know what I mean—at least according to their accounts.

A lot of the girls had parents who were professionals—doctors, lawyers, educators, and the like. I fit in that way, because Daddy was a politician and had his own business, and Mamma was a teacher, so pretty much everyone knew who we were. But we were just simple folks. We never behaved as though we were better than other people. We were very down to earth. Mamma would have spanked us good if we had behaved that way. Many of those girls, with a few exceptions, were some of the most unpleasant people I had ever encountered. They were stuck up and prideful. They weren't a lot of fun to be around.

You remember the way the McNair girls are expected to act. Mamma is the quintessential elegant lady, a Southern belle who raised us to be like her. She taught us to walk with our head held high. We had to walk around with books on our head to improve our posture. The goal was to walk so steady that the books would not fall off your head. Did she have you do that too? Mamma had in her mind the traditional image of debutantes coming out to society so they would be ready to meet and date nice eligible men. She wanted to make sure we had all the social graces a young woman was supposed to have.

Kim and I attended etiquette classes. We took piano, ballet, and sewing lessons so we could become good wives and elegant ladies. Mamma also taught us to cook. Daddy exposed us to other things like stained-glass-window-making classes, photography, and camping (which I hated), so we could be more well-rounded. We worked as summer pages in the state legislature when he served. Working in the legislature was fun, but I remember how cold it was in the chambers of the capital, especially in summertime. George Wallace was the governor again when we served. We got to meet him once, and Daddy had our picture taken with him. He was very nice to us.

Stephen Crutcher, our pastor's son at 16th Street Baptist, had been my "husband" in a Tom Thumb "wedding" (another Southern tradition) when we were four years old. From then on, the whole church considered us boyfriend and girlfriend. In high school, he was still my friend—mainly because we were both church members—but we did not attend the same school.

Mamma informed me that I would need an escort to all the debutante social affairs, so I asked Stephen to escort me to all the events including the ball. He was kind and said he would be happy to do it. The other girls also disliked me because I had someone to take me to all the events and they didn't, but according to Mamma, that was what you were supposed to do. It was weird to me because if they were supposedly so experienced with boys, why didn't they have one to escort them to events? Stephen and I were just friends, but they were supposed to have real "boyfriends." I really wished you had been alive during this time. You could have been a big help with navigating this whole experience.

Stephen Crutcher (my date at the debutante ball) and me. Photo by Chris McNair.

Daddy dancing with me during the father-daughter dance at the debutante ball. Photo from the Chris McNair Archives.

The whole year of being a debutante was filled with parties and activities. Each young lady had to host a party or a tea. We had to show what we had learned about putting together a social affair. I got together with nine of the girls and we had a huge party with a French theme. It was epic. Now I did enjoy that. Everybody that was anybody came. We also had a mother/daughter luncheon at, of all places, the Arlington Antebellum Home and Gardens. It's a nice place but come on, an Antebellum Home for a debutante event for a group of Black folks? Really? Seriously? I hope they have found some place more appropriate for African American girls to go now. At this luncheon we had our pictures made as a group. It is always a big deal every year that these photos appear in the newspaper several weeks before the ball.

There were going to be two main prizes at the end of the night of the ball: one was for the deb who made the best scrapbook of their lives and their future and the other was the debutante who could raise the most money. Back then I loved a challenge. I always wanted to win and be first in everything I did. I was not quite sure I could win with the scrapbooking; some of the other girls had some amazing ideas. But I thought I could surely raise the most money. I asked if the money went to underpriviliged kids to go to college. That's when they told me it was a fundraiser for the organization and not for a benevolent reason. That was so disappointing. I couldn't ask people for money for that. That really upset me. They said that each girl had to raise a minimum of $65.00 and that is what I did. My total contribution was $69.00 and not a penny more. The wind had gone out of my sails for this whole event at this point. I went through the motions through the ball, but that was it.

After a full summer and fall of activities, the gala grand finale ball took place in December. I looked pretty and Stephen looked great too. He was a very handsome young man. Mamma was elated, but Daddy hated every moment. He considered it, the debutante tradition, pretentious and vowed he would only stay for the father-daughter dance, then he was going home. All the rest of the family came: Dear Dear, Auntie Nee Nee, Kim, and Mamma.

It was a grand evening, but by the time the big day came I had had enough. Although some of the activities were fun, the event as a whole was a big letdown, like going to Midfield High. I thought I would make friends and I did make a few, but Daddy was right about the pretentiousness of a lot of the folks—not everyone but enough of them. I sure hope they have now restructured how they run the ball to make it be more meaningful. When the ball was over, all the girls and our dates went to Denny's for breakfast. The next morning, we were supposed to take a train ride to Tuscaloosa and back. Many of us had never been on a train before. It was the final social activity and probably would have been a lot of fun but I was done and didn't go. Plus we had to be up *really* early the next morning to catch the train after being up until 2:00 a.m. the night before. This was one of the many social activities they had planned for us.

Back to the day after the ball. I told Stephen that if he wanted to go on the train ride he was welcome to do so, but I was not going. When he took me home, I removed the dyed shoes that hurt my feet so badly and fell asleep still wearing my big white dress and tiara. I didn't wake up until noon the next day. I was tired and so disappointed in the whole thing that I had had enough. One more attempt to fit in had gone down the drain. It wasn't a total loss, however, because one of the girls, Rhonda Coman, became my college roommate. She has a great family with lots of sisters. We became very close, and her mom welcomed me like I was family.

Their household was the kind where you could just drop by unannounced, and I did often. They are great people. If Mamma knew how many times I showed up unannounced she would be very upset with me.

Another good thing happened years later. The Imperial Club, which put on the debutante ball, honored you and the other girls who were killed with you by designating every one of you as honorary debutantes. They invited us back to the ball in 2013, which was the fiftieth anniversary of your death, and gave each girl's family a wonderful tiara and a pair of long white gloves encased in glass with a plaque that had your name on it. It was a beautiful gesture and a loving tribute to you. I will never forget their kindness in doing that for you. We have the case in a prominent place in our home. That gesture sort of makes up for my less-than-stellar debutante experience.

I wonder if you would have been a deb. You might have been like Kim and Daddy, who thought, "This is stupid." By the time Kim was the age to be a deb, more and more girls chose not to "come out." The whole idea has lost a lot of its excitement and meaning. And like other traditions that seem somewhat out of place in the world today, perhaps that is for the best. They still have it every year. There are actually two other organizations that put a ball on each year as well.

Now I am ready to tell you about my time at college, which is going to take a few letters to complete.

Much love,
Lisa

Bama

Dear Denise,

I hate that you didn't get a chance to go to college. We often talk about where you would have gone and what you would have become. Some say you would have been a doctor. I think you would have been a lawyer. Daddy and some nice people in the community set up a scholarship fund in honor of all four of you on the twentieth anniversary of your deaths. It is called the 4 Little Girls Memorial Fund. They wanted a living legacy to all of you that would offer the opportunity for others to go to college, an opportunity that you were denied. The fund is for students going to Miles College, a historically Black college, or the University of Alabama at Birmingham (UAB), a state-run college that is predominantly white. Originally the fund supported students no matter where they went to school. But later they decided it should be for schools in town, one historically Black school and one traditionally white campus. Then, on the fiftieth anniversary of your death, a professor who directed the UAB gospel choir, Kevin Turner, wrote a song entitled "What Could Have Been." It is beautiful and is all about what you girls could have been today. I listen to it often. It always brings tears to my eyes. We had a big fundraiser for the fund and four young Black ladies sang the song at our event. It was magical. As I told you earlier, your life and your death have never stopped inspiring people.

After the bad time in high school, I was excited to go off to college. I applied to and was accepted to a number of colleges: Samford University, Birmingham Southern College, the University of Alabama, and Auburn Unversity, where Kim graduated. I chose and was accepted to the University of Alabama in Tuscaloosa. Roll Tide! Actually, I was always an Auburn University fan and wanted to go there. But during the summer between my junior and senior years, after I won student council president, I went to a weeklong workshop that was held on the campus of the University of Alabama on how to be an effective student council officer. Student officers from all over the state attended. We stayed in the dorms and had a great time.

I felt like a grown-up that week there all by myself. By the time I got through that week and had seen most of the campus, I was saying, "I'm going to Bama when I graduate!" I applied and you should have seen me the day I got my acceptance letter. Mamma wanted me to go to Samford because it was a small Christian college in Birmingham and she wanted me to be close to home. Daddy was all about me going to Alabama and couldn't wait for me to go there. It later dawned on me what a huge deal it was that I was accepted to Alabama. I had completely forgotten about George Wallace's "Stand in the Schoolhouse Door" to prevent the admission of Black students in the 1960s.

Just the thought of going to Alabama was liberating. At eighteen years of age, I was still desperately trying to find myself, along with the happiness and comfort I had when I went to Advent. I went to Bama and felt like this was going to be the place for me, my real coming-out party. Alabama was big and there were opportunities to meet so many new friends—Black people like me, and white friends as well. I could have rich white friends, poor white friends, rich Black friends, and poor Black friends, and even friends from other countries. I do love all types of people and making new friends is exciting for me. I was pumped and ready to go!

I guess that was another good thing that came from my time at Midfield: it taught me to appreciate folks from all walks of life. I would not have appreciated that had I not spent time with the students there. Before that, I held an elitist attitude, but I learned it takes all kinds to make a world and everyone has value. For that reason, I am grateful for my Midfield years, as hard as they were. Also, my involvement with student government got me to Alabama, so that was another plus.

Everyone was at Bama for the same purpose: to get an education and to start a new life. I was excited about the freedom I was going to have to come and go and do what I wanted. It wasn't that Mamma and Daddy were that strict; it was just time for me to guide my own ship, so to speak, and I was ready—although I had already experienced some measure of adult-type freedom. I had been working a job since I was fourteen, so when I wasn't at home or school, I was working. I had a super job at the Greater Birmingham Convention and Visitors Bureau, and that allowed me to go many places and meet lots of people. Part of my job was to know about all the attractions and hotels in the area and to be able to give good directions to visitors to Birmingham. It was an awesome place to work.

Rooming with Rhonda from the debutante experience was fun. I arrived at school a week ahead of time. Daddy had bought me a car, but my parents wouldn't let me take it to Bama until after I came home for Labor Day. So Mamma and Daddy dropped me off, and Daddy said Mamma cried all the way home. I worked all summer, had saved my money, and had purchased everything I was going to need. My Bama experience did start out well. I had a great time and made a lot of friends, white friends and Black friends, just as I had planned. The problem was that school was more difficult than I had ever anticipated. I was always afraid that I would have trouble in college. I can read but I read slower than most people. I have to take my time so that I read the words in order. I think I have dyslexia, but I have not been officially diagnosed. Once I read something, I have wonderful comprehension, but it takes me a very long time. It can be embarrassing sometimes.

My real college major was trying to find myself and where I fit in with the Black and white worlds. I spent more time working on that and on trying to date than doing the homework after class, and that was a problem. I was also trying to change the world, so I got involved wherever I could. I was on the council for my dorm. I was an SGA legislative associate, which meant I lobbied the legislature on the school's behalf. They wanted me because Daddy was a legislator. I was also volunteering for the Mondale/Ferraro presidential campaign, and I was part of the Black Student Union and the Baptist Student Union.

My life was very social. I went to all the Black frat parties and went to football games, but I didn't do a lot of homework. Procrastination is an issue for me; was it for you? After my first semester, I was placed on academic probation. Mamma and Daddy were unhappy with me and insisted I secure the services of tutors—as many as needed. They were used to me being an A and B student.

I wish someone would or could have seen where my head was at and put me on the right path. From my first days of college, I was obsessed with trying to figure out who I was, what group I fit in best with, how I was supposed to act, and how I should navigate this Black and white world. It was on my mind every day. And by this time finding a boyfriend was also a main priority. I guess everyone at Bama was trying to date but it was a mission for me. I didn't date in middle school, and not in high school either. I thought the debutante thing was going to open a door, but that was all a joke. When I met someone, I was always thinking, "Does he like me?" Before my sophomore year, I went home for the summer, worked my job, bought a whole new wardrobe, and got serious about makeup for the first time. I looked and dressed more like the other girls, but I was still very awkward. I guess you could say I was more of a girl nerd and I found it hard to fit in. So that year, with the help of some friends, I had a full makeover. For the first three or four months of my sophomore year, I got up every day to put on full makeup. That took a lot of time, time I should have devoted to my studies.

Another advantage of going to Alabama was that I thought I could finally have anonymity. No one was going to know I was Lisa McNair whose sister was killed in the bombing and whose father was a politician. I was going to start with a clean slate and be my own person. I was excited about that.

School started in August, and the twentieth anniversary of the bombing came about three weeks after I was in school. There was a lot of national attention because of the anniversary's significance. The folks from NBC called Daddy and asked him to make an appearance on *The Today Show*. I had three weeks of anonymity, but once Daddy was on national television, everyone at school knew who I was. Yet my "fame" and the show did help me find someone special.

One day, a student came to my door and introduced himself as Gerald Hamilton from the Student Government Legislative Association. That organization lobbied the legislature to secure funding for the university. Gerald had come to ask if I would serve on that committee. Did I mention he was white, and handsome? I was instantly taken with him.

I knew they were using me because of my access to Daddy and his connections, but I figured, "Okay, I want to have access to something too." They wanted to use me, so I would use them. When I agreed to serve, Gerald invited me to their club's first meeting of the year. It was held on the weekend; he told me he had to go home that weekend but that I should look for another student, the guy who ran the club, tell him who I was, and that Gerald had sent me. Forget the meeting, I instantly had a crush on Gerald. He was cute and so nice and polite. He had a dry sense of humor that made me laugh. We became fast friends.

Days later I went to the meeting Gerald told me about. Of course, as often happened, I was the only Black person in the room. This was the early 1980s. Things were intergrating but there were still few Black folks in all aspects of white-dominated businesses and organizations. Because of Daddy we were often asked to be part of organizations that had never had a Black person participate before. We were often the token. I was ok with that because if I got in, I was going to bring more Black folks in with me. Mamma and Daddy had told us to do just that. We were not to be selfish with our new opportunities. We had to make the way for other folks who may not have access as we did.

I noticed that everyone was giving me strange looks, asking with their eyes,

"Who is that Black girl and and why is she here?" At the end of the program, I was supposed to meet up with this guy. Most people were treating me like I was not even in the room. They totally ignored me, but I pressed on to find the person Gerald wanted me to meet. When I did, I extended my hand and introduced myself. The scenario changed quickly when they found out who I was, and I was then welcomed into their group of student politicos.

After that, Gerald and I formed a friendship and I fell for him in a profound way. I started working on committees and doing things with him, even though he was seeing someone else. Gerald was from the area outside Birmingham called Huffman, which is kind of a blue-collar area. He was a smart kid, got accepted to Bama, and pledged a fraternity, which made him part of the university establishment. I wanted to be with him, but my problem then was that I wasn't the kind of girl who asked a guy out on a date. More important, I was Black and he was white. Most important, he was unavailable!

I had all that going on and was still not doing a good job with my homework. In other words, I was flunking out of school while trying to find myself. I was making a huge mess of it all, and Mamma and Daddy were terribly displeased with me because of my grades. Finally, at the end of my first semester of my sophomore year, the university sent me home on academic suspension. That is their standard procedure for students who don't do well for three consecutive semesters. It's funny when I think of it: I guess the university didn't want to waste any more of our parents' money. It seemed to me at the time that they would let you stay as long as your money was good. I could apply to come back after sitting out one semester.

This was devastating, but I had no one to blame but myself. The crazy part about it is I don't think anyone could have stopped me from running into that brick wall. Counselors had talked to me. I had tutors. Mamma and Daddy were always scolding me. But I was in a zone, and it would be years before I got a handle on it. The suspension was a terrible shock, but it didn't automatically make me change.

At first, I wanted to die and literally wanted to kill myself. Not only was I dismissed from the school I loved, but I was going to have to tell the guy I was madly in love with that I had flunked out of school. What would he think of me then? He was no longer seeing that girl and was free to date me if he wanted. But who was I kidding? This was 1986 and he was white and I was Black. Even if he wanted to, it was a very taboo thing to do in the South. It would never have happened. At this point in my life I didn't know anyone other than people on television who dated interracially.

I went from being the golden child who was a good student in high school and who won awards, someone the whole family was proud of, to someone who flunked out of college. It was just awful, and I didn't know how to make it right. I packed all of my things to go home for Christmas because I knew I would not return. I would have to sit our parents down and tell them what I had done. That was going to be horrible!!!

Another thing that happened at Bama is that some of my Black friends at the time weren't cool with me being so close with white people. I'll give you an example: I was friends at Bama with two guys who were roommates, one Black and the other white. The Black guy was friendly and flirtatious, but none of us were in a serious relationship with him. His white roommate would hang out with us from time to time. One evening, all of us went to dinner, and I was sitting in a booth when the white guy put his arm across the back of the booth behind me.

It looked like he had his arm around me, but he didn't; nor was I bothered by it. After all, he was a friend of mine. Later, I caught all kinds of hell from his Black roommate for allowing the white guy to do that. My Black friend said that he had liked me, but when I let his roommate do that, he no longer wanted to have anything to do with me. His words really hurt mostly because I felt they were so unnecessary. We can do and say some silly, hurtful things as human beings to our fellow humans.

I wish you had been around then. I needed a big sister to talk to, on whose shoulder I could cry. Perhaps you would have had words of wisdom that would have set my thinking straight about where my priorities should have been. Alas, it was not to be, and I had to go home with more emotional baggage than I first brought to Bama. Life wasn't fair and I was about to find out that it would get worse before it got better.

I miss you,
Lisa

Suicidal Thoughts

Dear Denise,

While I was eligible to return to the University of Alabama, Daddy was done. He was so disappointed in me that he was not giving me another chance at Bama. He wanted me to pull my grades up at home at a local junior college. I didn't want that. I wanted to go back to Bama and give it another try. I felt I could work hard and really make it happen this time. I tried to get back for several years. I would have had to pay for it myself. That was harder than I thought. Daddy wasn't going to give me a dime. I even tried to join the army reserves, but they just laughed at me. They said I weighed too much. That didn't help my self-esteem either. After a while I had to realize that my career at Bama was over. My college adventure there had ended in failure, and I had to return home in disgrace.

I told Gerald about my suspension before I told our parents. He was really sweet about it. He didn't make me feel ashamed of myself but was very encouraging. He had just run for student body president of the campus and won. He was going to appoint me to a position in his administration. As an African American I would have been able to really make a difference for my people. I was going to use that opportunity to bring more Black students into student government. Since he couldn't give me that position, I named several of my Black friends that I wanted him to reach out to and offer them positions. And he did. He hugged me and wished me well. We both had tears in our eyes. He told me to please stay in touch and we have over the years. I never told him how much I loved him. I headed home to Birmingham. I cried all the way home. It was devastating. My heart was just broken. I had so much discomfort with who I was to begin with, and on top of that I was someone who didn't seem cut out for college. I felt like a failure. It's odd to look back on it now. It wasn't really the end of the world, just a very bad time. All I had to do was make a shift to study harder and stay focused, but I guess there was too much in my head at that time. I just could not pull it together to get it done.

I still had the job that Daddy had gotten me when I turned fourteen, at which I had worked every summer, Christmas, Thanksgiving, and spring break. When I came home for Christmas break, the receptionist had resigned. It was a gift from God. I asked the executive director if I could have that job. I had already performed the receptionist's duties when she went on breaks, so I was familiar with all the responsibilities. Since I had to sit out a whole semester, I needed a job and something to do every day besides be depressed that I flunked out of school. He agreed to give it to me, and I secured that job before I told our parents about school. I felt I needed to have something positive to tell them before I broke the bad news. They were terribly disappointed and didn't speak to me for a couple of days. Our house was a sad place to be.

I spent the next few years working at that job, trying to get back to Bama. Daddy said he wasn't spending any more money for my education. I thought that was a mean thing for him to say and do. After that, he did help get me into a junior college here in Birmingham, where I took a few classes. After I got a couple decent grades from there, I transferred to UAB, which is a four-year college here in Birmingham. Daddy was still angry. He refused to pay for that, so I had to pay for my own schooling.

While I was at UAB, I was spiraling out of control, like a person on drugs. I was depressed every day. I was still going to church, but it didn't mean anything. I was contemplating ways to kill myself, and how to do it correctly and not botch it. I was still in love with Gerald and would drive to Tuscaloosa to hang out with him and my friends.

I was working and making money, but at that point I had some credit cards and was running up my balances. Even when I tried to return to Bama a couple of semesters later and room with a friend of mine, I didn't have the money to do it.

I was going to UAB and working, but I was flunking out of UAB faster than at Bama. I went from golden child to a zero overnight. A friend from Midfield named Octavia also went to UAB. We started hanging out with each other, going to parties, and having a good time. She was a lot of fun to hang out with and didn't judge me for what happened at Bama. Then she got into some kind of academic trouble too, and we were both confronted with our need to get our acts together. I was lost and unable to figure it out. People characterized me as one of the most fun, happy, and loving people they had ever met, and every day I wanted to die. I just couldn't see any light at the end of this long, dark tunnel. I didn't understand why God had me in this place with no apparent way out. If there was one, I didn't see it. I guess you could say I was full of pride, too. I could have just worked and not worried about college for a while. But I wanted to go to college like all of my other friends. I felt it was shameful not to graduate from college when everyone I knew was doing that. Hindsight is twenty-twenty. I wish I knew now what I knew then. I wish someone had steared me toward a trade school. No one made that an option at all, but I was good with my hands and fixing things. I almost took small-engine repair in high school but dropped that class for a cooking class when I realized I was going to be the only girl there. I wish I had been brave enough to stick with it. I could have been a plumber or an electrician and probably made as much if not more money than my peers. I plan to go to plumbing school in the next year. I don't care what people think now.

Sadly by this time I was so depressed I could not turn it around. I had figured out how I was going to kill myself but had not determined when I was going to do it. On the drive to the Bama campus, the road was very dark at night and there were dozens of places to ride off the side of the road. Some places were very deep and a car could go down there and not be found for days. That is how I was planning to do it. At the same time, I was plagued with guilt: How was I going to do that to Mamma when she already lost a child? At that point, I was so miserable that it didn't really matter much to me. It took all I had to get up in the morning and go to work. It was like I couldn't breathe and had to fight for each breath. It was like a heavy black cloud was weighing me down. The Bible does say, "Weeping may endure for a night, but joy comes in the morning." That much is true. The sunlight came in my bedroom strong each morning and there were days that that would help me get out of bed. But if the day was overcast it was terribly hard. The fall was awful and nighttime was the worst. Depression and anguish were choking me, and I didn't know how I could survive it. Nobody knew all this but me, because I couldn't really share it with anyone. I didn't know anyone who could relate to my plight. Not only was I depressed about school and my finances, but there was still the issue of fitting in in the Black or white world. I guess it was like being a child of mixed-race parents and having to choose an identity. I wasn't mixed but I was just as torn up inside.

I did share some things with my friends. They were great, but in the cold silence of my nights, I was all alone. A heavy cloud of shame, sadness, and depression weighed heavily on my mind, but I was good at covering it up. If you had known me then, you would never have realized what I was going through unless I had told you. My job in life was always to be the happy one, make people smile.

That is kind of why I am here, if you think about it. Mamma and Daddy and the family lost you, and then I came to bring joy again. I didn't want to bring anyone down, so I did not share just how miserable I was.

I finally did confide in our first cousin Rodney, who lived in California and was a year or two younger than me. We would occasionally call and talk to each other about our lives, our parents, dating, and things like that. It started as most converations do with teenagers: complaining about life, when actually neither of us had anything to complain about. Rodney also had some problems in school. We talked at night when I couldn't sleep because it was earlier on the West Coast and I would not be waking him up. I remember very well that I called him on the night I intended to kill myself, perhaps hoping he would talk some sense into me, or maybe just to say good-bye. He talked me off the proverbial ledge, staying on the phone from about midnight until it was time to go to work in the morning.

It's funny how God uses people to help you who you least expect. Rodney was a lot of fun, but he was not usually very serious. He was always talking about girls and sex, so I didn't think he was very deep, but he was funny and made me laugh. That night, I found out how wrong I was. As he talked to me, he seemed ever so right about prayer, being spiritual, loving God, having faith, and maintaining hope. He encouraged me, telling me I was special, smart, and attractive. I could not believe that all of this encouraging counsel was coming from Rodney because, if you polled all the cousins, we would have told you that Rodney was one of the flakiest people we had ever met. That night he showed another side of himself. He saved my life that night, and I will always love him for it.

I guess that night I had hit rock bottom, because college started to get a little better after that. I realized I needed to make my life work, somehow; I had so much more to live for. I fought that gorilla of sadness and depression. With God's help, I found scripture verses to meditate on and Rodney called and checked on me often. I was determined never to sink so deep into that hole of sadness again.

We have another first cousin (we now have a total of thirty-two first cousins) who lives close by and is fifteen years younger than me. He's incredibly smart and gifted with a high IQ. When he got into high school, he started having the same issues that I had faced: a lack of focus and trouble understanding his place in the world. Knowing he was smart his school suggested that he be tested. They found that he had the intellect of a genius. He wasn't unfocused; he was just bored. He needed more intellectual stimulation and to be taught in a different way. The only reason he daydreamed a lot was that his mind was moving faster than everyone else. A lot of things they said about him were things teachers had said about me over the years.

I went to the same place where he had been tested, paid to have my own battery of tests done, and discovered that I had a high IQ as well. That confirmation of my own intelligence made all the difference for me with school. It let me know that there wasn't anything wrong with me, which encouraged me in an amazing way. When I told Mamma about my results, she said, "Oh yeah, we knew that a long time ago." I thought, "That would have been good for you to tell me before now!" I felt as if I finally had the incentive and confidence to try harder. At least now I knew there was nothing wrong with my mind.

Now I knew I wasn't stupid. I might have been a procrastinator and unfocused, but I knew that I could do the work. At UAB, from that point on, I studied harder, was more focused, and pulled up my GPA. I learned to love myself, all of me—the fat girl, the slow reader, the person who got kicked out of school, the white girl, and the Black girl.

I was getting my head together, but there were still many challenges ahead.

Your loving sister,

Lisa

The Family Business

Dear Denise,

By the time I began to figure out my academic career, life was going well for me and I wasn't depressed or suicidal any longer. I dated a couple of nice men but nothing serious. I was doing well at my job and got a promotion that moved me to the UAB campus, which was convenient for my classes. By then, our sister Kim had graduated from Auburn University with a degree in fine arts painting.

Daddy wanted her to come into the family business. He wanted me to come too. I had resisted for years because I knew Daddy had a business he loved, but he never ran it well or seemed to earn much of a living from it. I didn't want to be broke all the time, but I started going there a couple evenings after work, just to help out. I thought that would stop him from pressing me to work there full time. Sometimes I would go to the studio during my lunch break to work on pictures, because digital cameras were becoming common and I could edit pictures using a program called Photoshop. I won't even try to explain the computer and how that has changed our lives.

I had a talent for restoring old photos and saw how money could be made doing that. For years, Daddy had been saying he wanted me to come to work at his photography studio full time. I was doing well at school and was about to finish the degree I had been working toward for what seemed like forever. It was the mid to late 1990s at this time. Daddy put a lot of pressure on me to join him and even had some of his friends, many of them relative strangers to me, call to try and persuade me to come to work for him. The studio was not just for photography, but also had a one-hour photo lab and a custom framing shop. Daddy also thought he could add a graphic design service to the business that would do newsletters, ad layout, etc.

Eventually, I left my good job at the convention and visitors bureau that I had since I was fourteen years old to go work full time with my family. Daddy promised me I would get a salary and we would get paid every two weeks. It worked well for about a year or two, but it was not a good fit. I soon realized that I had made a bad decision. I thought I could surely work and go to school too, but one thing

I learned about running your own business is that it involves much more work than when you are working for someone else. I had about a year left toward earning my undergraduate degree but after I began working in the family business, I never went back to school. There just wasn't enough time in the day to do both work and school.

After I was there for a year or so, Daddy wanted to expand by adding an art gallery that would double as a banquet facility. He was trying to get the money for the art gallery for Kim, since she had majored in fine arts painting. This would be a place for her to show her work and the work of other artists. He also wanted it to display his own photographic work. He has a collection of historic photos from the Civil Rights Movement; many of them depict famous people like Dr. and Mrs. Martin Luther King Jr., Reverend Ralph Abernathy, Reverend Fred Shuttlesworth, Rosa Parks, Diane Nash, James Bevel, and Andrew Young. Also other celebrities of the time: Jackie Robinson, Gregory Peck, Ethel Waters, Mary McLeod Bethune, and John Lewis, just to name a few. But he couldn't raise the money. No banks would loan him money because of his credit history. So he ended up taking on some of his close friends as investors to help him build the gallery. Those investors got him into big trouble, which I will tell you about in another letter.

The business wasn't doing great even before all that drama occurred with building the gallery. Right before we started to build, we were just about at the break-even point. We should have kept going like that to gain more stability for about two or three more years. Kim and I helped bring a more stable business model to the company. Daddy had a great concept for his business, but he was not good at managing money. A business must make money; it's not there to inflate or massage someone's ego. It must be run on sound financial principles. When it's poorly run, it's bad for the owners and the employees who are depending on the business for their livelihood. Kim and I tried to get him to slow down and rethink his plan but he was determined to proceed. I have learned that to be that headstrong about something without looking at all the facts is not wise.

Daddy made a lot of bad decisions where the business was concerned. After years of watching the business sink and Daddy not listen to reason I had to get out. I worried and prayed a lot about it. I talked to Mamma about it, but Mamma is Daddy's biggest champion and has always been there for him. She always believed in him, even when he was wrong. She advised me to stay because he needed me. She is the best wife in the world. No man could ask for a better helpmate.

I had a lot of ideas that could have helped the business, but Daddy wanted to implement almost none of them. If I had stayed, it would have not been in anyone's best interests. Daddy needed to see the error of his ways, and I needed to have a regular income and to relate once again to my family as just family and not business partners. It is hard to work with family because often the same dynamics that are in a family are in the business as well, and it isn't conducive to good business practices.

One morning I was watching Bishop T. D. Jakes on television. He is a nationally known minister who can be heard on the radio and seen on TV. He was talking about the number seven representing the number of completion in the Bible. I noted that I had been at the studio seven years and made up my mind then and there that I was leaving. I had been praying and looking for a sign, and that was it. I told Daddy and Kim later in the day that I was leaving to get a job. I explained that I hadn't been paid regularly for the previous two years and needed income. I stayed until I found employment.

Leaving Daddy's studio was one of the hardest things I have ever done. I really wanted to stay and try different business practices to see if there were things we could have done to improve the business, but in the end, Daddy had the last word and would not listen to anyone. I don't know if you got to see that side of Daddy. Some folks just can't admit they are wrong—and even if they do admit it, they can't seem to make the necessary effort to change. They would rather do things the wrong way than admit defeat. I had to make a living, but fortunately, I was still living at home and had a roof over my head. We had decided to pay the staff and not ourselves because we needed them and they needed to make a living. I had no income coming in from work, however; only some from rental property I owned, and even that depended on whether or not the tenants paid on time.

Daddy, Mamma, and Kim were very upset with me, but by that time I had spent all my savings. The first thing I did was go to a temporary employment agency to find something quick that would make money. I also sent my resume to a woman who had founded an organization called Hand in Paw. I was serving on their board of directors at that time. What I didn't know was that she was looking for an executive assistant. She hired me and I was there for more than fifteen years. I love this organization! More on what I did there in a later letter.

I have focused on my journey and pain up to this point, but it's time we returned to your life for a few letters. I want you to know about what this city and country have been like since your death and the response to it. I think you will be surprised.

Much love,
Lisa

The Trials

Dear Denise,

I knew early on in life that if I did something wrong, I would be punished. There would be consequences, even if they were only Mamma giving me a whooping or taking away certain privileges. It was some time later when I learned about the American justice system. People who commit crimes usually go to prison or suffer some other consequence for their actions, but first they go through a trial with a jury of their peers who will determine their fate. So it was quite a surprise to learn that the men who had been accused of murdering you and the other girls had not been arrested, tried, or convicted, and were serving *no* jail time. I could not understand why there had been no investigation and why no one had been arrested for your murder.

What seemed even crazier and more wrong to me about your death was that our parents were not constantly fighting and crusading for this next step toward justice. They seemed to have made peace with the past. I later grew to understand that, at that point in history, there was little our parents could do because of the way things were for Black folks in America in general and Alabama in particular. It seemed like such a huge injustice to me, and of course it was.

Why was it that Black folks were not supposed to expect justice, not even to mention it, or ask for it—let alone actually receive it? Even in the 2010s and '20s, the issue of Black justice remained unresolved, especially regarding police killings of Black people. We've come a long way, but still have a long way to go.

In 1977, something that I thought would never happen, happened. One man was brought to trial for your murder! I have already mentioned him to you: his name was Bob Chambliss, nicknamed "Dynamite Bob" because he had a reputation for setting off bombs in the Birmingham area. From what our parents told me some time later, the FBI investigation originally identified five suspects who helped make and plant the explosive device that killed you: Robert Chambliss, Bobby Frank Cherry, Tommy Blanton, Herman Cash, and Charles Cagle.

In 1977, Bill Baxley, Daddy's friend whom he met while serving in the state legislature, was the Alabama attorney general. He mentioned to Daddy that he wanted to reopen the case and prosecute Robert Chambliss because he felt that Chambliss would be the easiest to convict. He came to Daddy with this idea because he thought it was a good time to do it. Daddy was not sure that anyone else would try if it didn't get done during Bill's time in office. Daddy agreed to let him try the case.

I was thirteen years old in the fall of 1977, and this was an exciting event for me. I was glad to know that justice was going to have a chance to prevail. Of course, at age thirteen, I was still a child and not allowed to go to the trial. I could hardly wait to come home every evening and find out how it went in court.

Kim and I were sheltered from many things in the outside world while we attended Advent. During the time of the trial, however, Mamma and Daddy were concerned for our security while we were in school. They were trying not to alarm us, but, as I've already told you, I remember the teachers paying special attention to us during that time.

When the trial ended, the jury received their instructions to go and decide on a verdict. We all waited anxiously for their ruling. Black people had lost many battles in court when we were up against white people. It was easy to think that we could not actually win a court case in America, especially down South, even when the facts were clear and indisputable. Finally, we got word that the jury had reached a decision, and they came back with a guilty verdict. I was elated, shocked, and amazed all at once. It showed that justice could happen in America and how far we had come: a white man in the South *could* be convicted of a crime against a Black person.

As happy as I was, I had one lingering question: What about the other men who helped Chambliss? Would they be tried for their murderous crime? Daddy told me that he didn't know if or when those other men would ever be brought to justice. I was sad to hear that, especially on the heels of such a victory. I did hope that one day those responsible would be brought to justice. What I learned later is that Bill Baxley was criticized severely for opening up this case.

Little did I know that it would be more than twenty years before that hope would be realized. It came about through a series of events that thrust our family once again into the national spotlight. That process started in 1996 when Spike Lee, a Black movie director and producer, contacted Daddy wanting to do a movie about you and the other three girls killed in the 16th Street Baptist Church bombing. He knew about Daddy because Daddy had often been the unofficial spokesperson for the families about the bombing. Also, Spike's father was from Alabama and he had family here.

Daddy had channeled his grief about your death and used it as motivation to bring the white and the Black communities together. His efforts toward mutual understanding and cooperation were common knowledge, and he was regularly commended for it. He was also more accessible in public and to the press than some of the family members of the other girls. After your death, Daddy pleaded for calm and asked that there be no retaliation. He wanted us, as the Black community, to take the high road and we did.

Spike had written Daddy in the fall of 1984 about the possibility of doing the movie. At the time, Spike was a film student. I don't think Daddy followed much pop culture back then. I was twenty at that time, but Daddy was almost sixty. The most television I had ever seen him watch was the show *60 Minutes*, the news, *Hee Haw* on Saturdays with the family, and programs on our local PBS affiliate. And he almost never went to the movies. When Spike wrote, I was excited, but Daddy wasn't feeling it, so he didn't respond to his letter.

Years later, Spike contacted Daddy again when he came to Alabama for a film festival. He was better known at that time and well established as a noted movie director. I was excited about meeting him, but by then I no longer felt that a movie was a good idea. I didn't want Hollywood to sensationalize or change your story, as seemed to happen with other "true life stories." Your story and those of the other girls and their families were too important and personal to be told lightly or sensationalized.

I thought a documentary would be the best way to share with the world the lives of Carole, Cynthia, Addie Mae, and you. I wanted a true story, one that captured each of your lives in all of their potential and richness, and what losing each of you meant to each family.

I have to run right now, but I will pick up the rest of the story in the next letter, and then explain how the movie helped bring some of your other killers to justice, almost forty years after your death.

Love,
Your Sister Lisa

4 Little Girls

Dear Denise,

Spike never gave up on the idea of doing a movie about you and the girls. In time, Spike was invited as a special guest to Birmingham for a small film festival. Daddy and I were scheduled to photograph a wedding the same Saturday as the festival. Several people had mentioned that Spike wanted to see Daddy and speak with him. We were a little skeptical and felt if Spike really wanted to talk to us, he would call us.

We called Mamma before we came home from the wedding, and she informed us that Spike had indeed called and asked if Daddy would please come downtown to the hotel where the evening banquet for this festival was taking place. As tired as we were from the wedding, we went over to the hotel. The event was still going on and as soon as we entered the room, they notified Spike that we had arrived.

We met with Spike, of all places, smack dab in the middle of the hotel lobby with his bodyguards around us, along with many onlookers who walked by pointing and staring. Why we didn't meet in his room to get away from the crowd I will never know, but it was Spike's idea to meet there. I was not asked to be a part of the conversation, so I sat a few feet away. I wanted to interrupt and say, "We will only do it if it is a documentary," which I did blurt out after Daddy called me over to them as they finished their conversation.

When I got back in the car, I grilled Daddy and demanded that he repeat the entire conversation. Daddy told me a little, but I know he left out quite a bit. He did say that Spike was still interested in making a movie about you and the other girls killed in the bombing. He said Spike would be back in Alabama soon to start the process.

The thought of a movie about you was thrilling, but I didn't let myself get too excited. I didn't want it to be a movie that told a Hollywood version of what had happened on September 15, 1963. I kept reminding Daddy that it should be documentary about the real lives of the four girls. Spike and Daddy spoke again and they decided that it would indeed be a documentary, one that would allow the integrity of your lives to be maintained and the story to be told accurately. Daddy made it seem like it was his idea, but I knew it was mine.

The filmmaking began and, although it was exciting, it was also quite sad. The movie was Spike's first time shooting a documentary. Spike came down to Birmingham several times before filming and even stayed at our house once. He began doing research for the documentary, meeting with our family as well as with the other girls' families, a number of local folks who knew the girls, and some key figures in our city and state. Several decades had passed since the bombing and many folks had not really talked about what happened on that tragic day. It was odd how we had all been so quiet and hesitant to share how we felt.

As fate would have it, Daddy is a professional photographer and had captured practically every moment of your life on film. When Spike came to our house and began going through our family pictures, he was giddy with excitement—not an emotion I normally would have used to describe Spike Lee. He began to see how the documentary would come together and looked forward to looking at more pictures Daddy had taken.

Until Spike Lee entered our lives, I didn't realize how much I didn't know about the bombing and your life. You were the only child of our parents at the time of your death. Finding the pictures for Spike and gathering other materials proved stressful. Suddenly I viewed Daddy in a way that I had never seen him before. He was always the face that the media sought out when the anniversary of the bombing came around. He spoke calmly, almost in a matter-of-fact manner. For this task, however, he could not handle going through your things or reliving memories of you—the things you did, the places you went, the things you said. It was humbling to realize that although he always seemed so strong, he was deeply affected.

Mamma and I continued to look through your pictures and cry, sometimes together, sometimes apart. Mamma looked in one room and I looked through items in another. When we looked at photographs or other items together, Mamma would tell me stories about your life. It helped me to feel closer to you. I found it odd that I would cry because I am not much of a crier.

I never got to meet you; I never knew you to form a relationship with you, but I felt Mamma and Daddy's pain and I couldn't help but wonder what it must have been like to have your only child killed so tragically and for no reason. I imagined what it was like to have you flitting around the house calling out, "Mamma this" or "Daddy that," sharing all that happened in your day at school or with your friends . . . and then all at once coming home and hearing a deafening *silence*—no more hugs or kisses, no more stories being told of your day at school or playing with friends. The pain of that must have been unbearable.

Preparing for the movie gave us a chance to talk about you, and I learned some things about you I didn't know. I heard our parents tell stories about you and how you were strong, bold, and defiant, but fair. That would make you more like Daddy, because Mamma tended to be sweet and passive. Sometimes I think you would have been a good politician or a magnificent lawyer. I heard stories that you had a heart of compassion and kindness. You were socially active and did things like raise money for muscular dystrophy by having a fair in our front yard. You gathered all of the children in our neighborhood to participate.

There was also a story about you and a girl named Martha who wanted to be in the neighborhood club. Martha didn't have very much money. Not only that, but Mamma said that Martha also had dark brown skin. Several of the girls in the neighborhood didn't want Martha to be in the club for those reasons. You were angry with them for their prejudice and adamant that Martha be welcomed into the club. You even offered to pay her dues. It was either that, or you were going to leave the club.

Martha was made a member because you saw a wrong and made it right, and you didn't care who was offended. If you only knew how much your life and death helped to correct a bigger wrong and helped to create a new Birmingham in a new South. I have the privilege of living in the world that you helped make after you were gone, and today your memory is held in high esteem because of the price you and others paid for our freedom.

I imagined Mamma and Daddy talking with friends who had children and the friends sharing their family stories, but Mamma and Daddy having no stories to share. That must have been devastating. I know how much Mamma wanted children and loves young ones to this day. I know how she loved on us, and I can't imagine the object of that love being taken away so suddenly and violently. I often wonder how she and Daddy stayed sane. I am not sure that I would have been able to be so strong. I know I love the Lord and He loves me, but I don't know if I could come back from something like that and go on to raise two more daughters. For that, I will always applaud them.

They taught us to love everyone and not to harbor hate in our heart. For the most part, Kim and I have led our lives that way. They also taught us to be strong, no matter what. Sometimes when I am down or frustrated, I think of Mamma and Daddy, and I press on. I have to press on because if they could, surely I can.

Spike interviewed lots of our friends and family, even Kim and me, but unfortunately our parts got cut from the film. I listened in on his interview with Mamma and Daddy. I heard most of Daddy's interview. He was his usual cool and collected self; he showed very little emotion and even made jokes during a few lighter moments. Mamma, however, was a different story. Daddy had sheltered Mamma from most of the press for years, especially when it came to you. She didn't mind not being in front of the camera all those years. I was glad Spike interviewed her. Our mother's voice needed to be heard; that pain that can only be expressed by a mother needed to be felt by all who watched the film.

Spike interviewed her in our dining room. I sat on the floor in the corner of the room. I didn't know it at first, but everyone must be absolutely quiet while they are filming. During one of the shoots I had to go across the street and ask the neighbors to turn down their car radio while they were washing their car. The recording devices were so sensitive that we also had to turn the air conditioner off.

I knew that Mamma would probably cry, and I wanted to be in the room with her for moral support. I didn't want to be put out of the room while she was talking, but I felt like I was going to cry too. She spoke so eloquently during the filming. She showed the emotion you would expect from a mother who deeply loved her child and had her tragically taken away from her. Spike began by having her tell a little of how she and Daddy met. Later she described what you were like. He then asked questions about the day leading up to the bombing. The sound of her voice changed as she recounted the story of the evening before and the day of your death.

It's always been difficult for me to see Mamma cry, and this was probably the worst. I felt all her sadness and all her sorrow from that day as if it were happening to me at that moment, and it was gut-wrenching. I could barely breathe. I sat in the corner with tears streaming down my face. I wanted to scream and cry aloud. I was shaking, trying not to cry aloud; trying not to scream for the sheer agony of it all. Our mother is the sweetest person in the world—I know you know that—and for someone to hurt her like that is unthinkable. She got through it and did a wonderful job. I'll never forget that day as long as I live. To this day, I can't watch that part of the film. When I have to, I feel all of that pain all over again, I shake uncontrollably and weep from the depths of my soul. Sometimes I am asked to speak to a group and they want to watch the documentary with me and then have a question-and answer session with me following the film. If I can get by without rewatching it and just come back into the room after the film, I will.

The poster promoting the documentary film *4 Little Girls* about you and the other girls, directed by Spike Lee and produced by HBO. Spike did an amazing job on this documentary. People who had been silent for years were finally free to share the life stories of you, Addie Mae, Cynthia, and Carole, and how your death broke the hearts of folks in this community.

Sometimes that is unavoidable, which makes the Q and A very challenging. I often cry through most of it. I have found now that I am really exhausted the next day. It takes a whole lot out of me. To me, the interviews with the mothers were the most poignant moments in the entire documentary. This was probably the most that some of them had discussed the bombing in years, and I hope it was healing for them to do so.

Spike made this film in conjuction with HBO. When the film was released under the title *4 Little Girls*, it ran in theaters in a limited distribution throughout the country. There were special opening nights in some major cities, and Mamma and Daddy went to all of them. They would cry most of the time, and it was good for them, even cleansing. They met many stars at the screening in Hollywood, including Denzel Washington. Kim and I went to the one in Washington, DC, with them. We were in tears as soon as the opening credits began.

Here in Birmingham, the film premiered at the Alabama Theatre downtown, and they showed it for several weeks more in the smaller theater in the heart of our historic Black area of town. You would remember it as the only theater our people could go to when you were alive, the Carver Theatre. Today, it is known as the Carver Theatre and the Alabama Jazz Hall of Fame Museum, but now we Black folks can go to any theater we want—and we can go through the front entrance. The documentary got publicity nationwide and Daddy appeared with Spike on several national programs, including *The Today Show*, to promote the film.

As the national attention grew, one part of the story that stood out was that there were other bombers who had never been tried for the murders. If people in Birmingham were raising questions about them, I knew people all over the country surely were, as well. Why hadn't they been apprehended and brought to trial? Soon after the premiere here, the FBI in Birmingham, headed up by Rob Langford, reopened your case. This subsequently led to the indictment of Thomas Blanton and Bobby Frank Cherry. The other suspects, Cash and Cagle, had previously passed away.

By the time of their trial, I was older and I got the chance to see firsthand how a trial is run. Of course, this was no ordinary trial, for yours was no ordinary murder.

Love,
Lisa

Justice

Dear Denise,

As African Americans, we were accustomed to being disappointed when it came to matters left up to our court system involving justice for people of color. As an example, there was a string of bombings throughout the 1950s and '60s that led to Birmingham being nicknamed "Bombingham." To the best of my knowledge, no one from those bombings was ever arrested, let alone tried and convicted. For decades, that held true even for your high-profile death. What a travesty.

At times, white suspects were arrested for race crimes, but seldom would a jury of their white peers vote to convict them, even in the face of overwhelming evidence that pointed to their guilt. The courts had given us no satisfaction, so we as a people learned to put our trust in God, who is our Vindicator. It was always painful, however, not to be treated equally under the law, so I tried not to get my hopes up too high during any of the trials that involved your killers. I guess I had been conditioned to think that way.

I could not attend most of the Thomas Blanton trial. I was working in the family business and we were quite busy at the time. Kim attended with Mamma and Daddy while I held down the fort. Neither Kim nor I were there when the verdict came in and, for some strange reason, we were not looking for it on TV. We weren't aware that the jury could decide so quickly, but as soon as the jurors came back with a guilty verdict, our phone went crazy! I was shocked, and I couldn't believe it. A tear did come to my eye, and we all shouted, "PRAISE THE LORD!" Justice had finally been served after all those years after your death—thirty-eight, to be exact. Daddy and Mamma believed in the system and it finally worked.

It was another year before the Bobby Frank Cherry case went to trial. I was determined that I was going to be present for that one, and I did attend most of the trial. It was quite interesting to watch the proceedings. There were representatives from each of the four girls' families there. Mamma, Daddy, and I were there along with our Uncle Harold and Auntie Vivian (you remember our Dad's youngest brother and his wife), along with our first cousin Ava Denise McNair Story, who was named after you. She is Uncle James's daughter. He adopted her after you were killed because he loved you so much and missed you terribly. He and his wife had no kids. You have a very special place in her heart, since it was because of you that she was adopted, and Uncle James included your name in hers.

Cynthia Morris Wesley, who died with you that day, was also an adopted child, but her biological brother and sister attended and sat next to me. Their names were Eunice Davis and Fate Morris. Dianne Robertson Braddock, Carole Robertson's sister, and Mrs. Alpha Bliss Robertson, Carole's mom, were there too. June Peavey and Sarah Collins, two of Addie Mae Collins's sisters, were there as well. If there were more family members, I can't remember them. It was a long time ago. I told you about Sarah; she was in the bathroom with you girls when the bomb went off and she lost an eye. She too was a victim but had received much less attention than the four of you who died. She also testified at the trial.

Unlike courtrooms seen on TV, this courtroom was laid out differently. As spectators faced forward, the prosecution and the defense were in front of the audience on an elevated platform about three steps higher than the rest of us. It made it appear as if they were on a stage. The judge was the farthest away from us. The jury was on the right, facing the prosecution and defense tables. The spectators were not behind the lawyers' tables as you often saw on television.

I had two interesting experiences during the trial. Just outside the courtroom to the left was a private area comprised of small rooms with glass doors and windows that were not accessible to the public. One day during a break, I saw Bobby Frank Cherry with a family member holding hands and praying in one of the rooms with a big glass window. That surprised me and I had to stop and reflect on why they would be praying. He committed murder and he knew it. But I guess that would not stop his family from praying for him. It seemed very hypocritical to me. I didn't know what they were praying for, but it was insulting to think that they may have been praying for him to be acquitted when he himself knew he was guilty.

My second experience involved a restroom break. There were restrooms in the outer hallway where there was often a line when court was in recess. The prosecution lawyers, defendants, and all the defense lawyers exited to the left of the courtroom. Those of us in the family section would also exit to the left. If we had exited out of the back of the courtroom, we would have been barraged by the press. This area was secure and only those of us with the family, lawyers, and defendants were allowed in that area. It was off limits to the public.

I assumed that Bobby Cherry would have a totally separate area where he would enter and exit the courtroom, and we would be in another. But one day while waiting in the line to get down the hallway to the restrooms, I found myself standing right next to him. I did a double take and wondered why someone was dumb enough to let him be out there with the rest of us.

After I realized it was him, I thought, "Should I speak to him? Should I hit him? Should I curse him?" I thought about asking him why he hated Black people so much, and then telling him that I didn't hate him. When I studied him, he looked like someone's grandfather, which maybe he was. I chose not to say anything because I didn't know if it would jeopardize our case against him. I must admit that it was a strange wait for the restroom that I will never forget.

Doug Jones, who was the US attorney for our district at that time, was the lead lawyer for our side. He and his team had done an excellent job of research in preparation for this case. They were precise and detailed. One day, they showed pictures of the four girls when you were alive. Later they showed the morgue photos of you and the other girls. Thank God, he turned the projector away and the audience was not able to view them. I had seen them before in Spike Lee's documentary, and they were disturbing and upsetting to view. Doug Jones went on to describe the effects of having a bomb destroy your body. It was riveting.

At one point, I thought I was going to pass out. I could literally feel everything he described about the impact of the bomb on your body in my own body. From what he described, the force of the bomb possibly destroyed your insides and cut off your breathing before the blast and the bricks and mortar tore into your body. That was a bit too graphic for me, and I was unsettled for several days after hearing that. I still wonder how Mamma and Daddy could sit through that and not break down or cry out in grief—or at least faint. It was almost overwhelming to describe.

As the testimony went on, it was clear that Bobby Frank Cherry was a man with a lot of hatred in him. Family members even testified against him. His lawyers tried to mount a defense, but I think they knew they didn't have a leg to stand on.

After both sides had presented their cases, they each gave closing arguments. The judge gave instructions to the jury, which was a process that took far longer than I expected it would. Then it was the nail-biting time. You can never really tell what exactly each jury member heard and how they will decide. I prayed fervently that they would do the right thing and convict Bobby Frank Cherry for a crime that he clearly committed and for which justice was long overdue.

Once the jury came back with the verdict, the judge gave the courtroom instructions. I thought that was odd; I didn't see why I needed instructions. He warned that once the verdict was read, there were to be *no* outbursts in his court. I was bothered by that because after all this time, if Cherry was found not guilty, I wanted to yell, "Unfair!" and if he was found guilty, I wanted to shout, "Praise the Lord, Hallelujah. Thank You, Jesus!" They read the verdict and he was found guilty on all counts. I remained quiet on the outside, but I was shouting on the inside with tears flowing from my eyes.

I don't know if I can fully describe how I felt at that moment. In my mind I kept saying, "Guilty, guilty, guilty! Thank You, God! Thank You, Jesus!" As good as my life had been up to that point and as privileged as I had always felt, there was part of me that thought, "Well, you are Black and this is America, so they may not convict him." Justice had been denied for so long, but on that day, justice felt really good. I kept thinking, "You *can* be Black in America and get justice; justice does prevail."

I sat in my seat and cried. Tears flooded out of me and they kept coming for a long time. Someone was holding me; I finally looked to see that it was Cynthia Morris Wesley's sister, Eunice. I finally got the presence of mind to look over at Mamma and Daddy. Mamma was crying too, and Daddy was his stoic self. The judge allowed Bobby Frank Cherry to speak, and he said something crazy about it being a conspiracy, and blamed everyone but himself.

I looked over at Doug and the other prosecution lawyers, and they were all visibly moved. It touched me that they took that whole procedure so personally to cry when it was over. They just didn't shed a tear or two, they were visibly weeping. Then they came down off their platform and hugged all of us. This meant almost as much to them as it did to the families. I will never forget that, and I will be forever grateful. Doug Jones had put off his plans to run for the US Senate to finish procecuting these killers. Years later he would realize that dream and became the first Democratic senator from our state since his mentor, former senator Howell Heflin. We were so proud. He served our state well and with honor.

Afterwards we all walked out of the courtroom and made our way outside. The press was there in droves. Doug spoke briefly, as did some the other family members and one or two local people who were close to the families, and then we walked away. Mamma and Daddy said not one word to the press. That was interesting to me because I felt that, after all those years, that was the time to speak. It would have been nice if they praised God or thanked the lawyers, or done both. They could have also said that they knew the verdict would not bring you back but they were happy that justice was finally served. They just left with us, however, and never uttered a word to the press. I guess that is just how they wanted that to go.

I will never forget the whole trial experience. It will forever be a significant turning point in my life and in the lives of Black folks in Alabama. All three men were given life in prison. We had tasted justice and it was sweet. All three killers who were convicted of your murder died in prison. None of them ever acknowledged their guilt or repented for their actions as far as I know.

Blanton was the last one to die, in the summer of 2020. Several years before his death, he came up for parole. When we got the letter in the mail, I was shocked. I thought, "are they kidding? He was convicted to four life sentences. How can you get parole with that sentence?" There was practically a nation-wide response to learning of his possible release. People came from all over the country to his hearing. Thousands of letters were written to ask that he not be paroled. I made sure I attended the event and testified in front of the parole board. Blanton didn't show up and neither did anyone to speak on his behalf. What a terrible person he must have been that near the end of his life that no one cared for him enough to say a good word for him. That's a sad way to live. His parole was denied and he had another five years to come up for parole again. He did not live to see that day.

The year before Blanton died, I had thought about visiting him in prison. I always wanted to do it. Mamma used to always say she wondered why they hated us so since they were supposed to be Christians. She said she would like to ask the killers that question. I had spoken with Doug and another friend about getting me into the prison to visit him. I too wanted to just talk with him as one human being to another. I just couldn't believe that after getting to know me that he might not want to at least apologize. It is sad to think that someone could hold hate in his or her heart for that long. How could he stay locked up like that in his spirit? He could never be free that way. It is actually very sad. I hate I never made that connection with him.

Love you lots,
Lisa

Tracey

Dear Denise,

As I said earlier, I often wondered what it would be like to meet one of the Klansmen who were responsible for your death, or one of their family members, on the street one day. Since I grew up with white people all around me, went to school with them, and had them in our inner circle of family friends, that scenario would often cross my mind. What if I met one at school? What if I met one at my Daddy's photography studio? What if Daddy met one while he was serving in the state legislature? (Which I learned later he did—not someone who was actually indicted but someone who was a person of interest whom they could never get any evidence on. This person sat next to Daddy). What if there was a child of one of them who attended my ballet class?

Would they know who I was, and that my sister had been killed by their family member? Would they try to do more evil by killing me or harming my family or me? Would they admit who they were? Would they be remorseful? Would they cry? Would they ask for forgiveness? All kinds of things went through my mind. Birmingham is a large city but in degrees of separation it is very small. Everyone knows everyone, or at least knows someone you know. There is a small-town feel to this city sometimes. As the years went on, I stopped dwelling on that possibility, but it was always in the back of my mind.

Sometime in the early 2000s, I participated in something called a Walk to Emmaus. It is basically a four-day retreat sponsored by the Methodist church. I am a Baptist, but people from any denomination can participate. Several of my friends at the time were active in the Walk, and they sponsored my participation. It was a wonderful experience, and just what I needed. My life was stressful and difficult at the time, and I needed the four days away from my family and work. I was working at the family business at this time. The Emmaus ministry team was made up of nice, loving, God-fearing people who volunteered their time to put the weekend together. Once you participate in the Walk, you are asked to come back and volunteer your time when it is convenient for a future Walk weekend. It was a way to give back what you had received.

I was asked to come back and volunteer many times, and I did go back several times, but only for part of the weekend. One year they asked me to come back and stay for the entire weekend. My schedule was full because we photographed many weddings on weekends, and I knew that I would not be able to participate. I hated to keep saying no, however, so I asked my friend Mindy if she would mind going in my place. Mindy, who is white, had been on an Emmaus Walk many years before we met each other when she lived in another state. She was going through a difficult time, and I thought this might uplift her as well as fill my spot so they would not have a vacancy. Mindy agreed and attended a planning meeting for the retreat, which was a few months away.

Shortly after she left the planning meeting, she called me distressed and in tears. She could hardly compose herself to tell me what was bothering her. She asked if the planners of the event had told me that Tracey was going to be there? I told her that they did not, and I didn't know anyone by her real name ("Tracey" is a pseudonym). She was rambling at this point and I finally asked her to calm down and tell me who Tracey was. She said she was so glad that I didn't attend because one of the ladies there who was going to be a retreat speaker was this woman named Tracey, and she was the daughter of one of the original suspects in the bombing that caused your murder. She said, "Tracey, Tracey's daddy killed your sister." You can imagine how shocked I was; I wasn't quite ready for that. I also was glad I had not attended the meeting, because no one had mentioned that this lady was going to be there. "Surely they would not have let me walk into that without prior warning?" I thought.

Mindy went on to give me a summary of the story that Tracey shared with the planning committee, and it was quite moving. Tracey said that she had never shared her story before, even with her closest friends, but once she did, Mindy reported that there was not a dry eye in the meeting. All I could say again and again was, "Wow!" Mindy asked what I thought but I wasn't sure what to say or how to respond. What I had always dreaded had almost happened, as I suspected deep down inside that it would one day. As I said, Birmingham can be a very small city.

I didn't know whether to hate Tracey or not. My mother had always told us to love everyone, but this was different. What would my Black friends and family say if I forgave her and was kind to her? What did I really feel? Was I angry? Did I hate her? Would Mamma and Daddy want me to talk to her? How would Kim feel about it? Would she be upset that I spoke with her? The logical side of me said, "She didn't kill your sister. She was just a child herself when it happened." But my emotional side left me confused about how to feel. Somehow I knew that God would want me to give this woman a chance.

Usually I don't need much time to process my emotions. I am not an indecisive person, but this situation was going to take some time. I shared this story with several other friends via text message. Oh, you don't know what a text message is, do you? You only had an old-style black phone with a rotating dial on the front of it, attached to the wall. Well, we carry small portable phones with us everywhere we go now. They have screens like a television set, and we can make calls or send and recieve written messages on them.

Anyway, I took a poll among my friends as to what I should do. Some said they were glad I didn't go. Most of them asked, "What do your parents think?" I didn't tell Mamma and Daddy for a long time. They had suffered for so long, I wasn't sure they could take knowing about this. It was just too heavy. And besides, they were now suffering from Alzheimer's and dementia. Others said I should not meet Tracey. Many were concerned about my safety, and to be honest, I was too. What if this was an act on her part? What if she was a plant from the Klan and she was there to seek me out and harm me or my family? After a while, I let it rest and didn't think about it anymore.

Weeks went by and the retreat weekend took place. Mindy went and had a great time. I failed to mention that these retreats are very integrated, with both Black and white folks in attendance. It's a wonderful experience with everyone there so excited to be there to praise God. While Mindy was there, she informed Tracey that she and I were friends. Tracey told her she wanted to meet me. When Mindy told me that, I froze. That would be an intense moment, and I didn't know if I was ready.

Mindy explained to me that Tracey was now a child of God who happened to have a father who had been evil and angry. Then I got some other calls, emails, Facebook messages, and texts from women who were at the retreat whom I had known for a long time. They were also informing me that Tracey wanted to meet me. I agreed to meet, and Tracey and I planned and talked about doing it and could never seem to make it work. I guess it wasn't the right time.

I thought that maybe it would all end there, but it didn't. Something was in motion that could not be stopped, and it was an encounter that God wanted me to have. I have learned that racism dehumanizes everyone, both Black and white.

Some of our sick white brothers and sisters tried to make us less than human and, in the process, they became less than human themselves. If we were all going to live in this country together, we have to do the hard and painful work of reconciliation. It was my turn to contribute to the healing.

Love,
Lisa

Reconciliation

Dear Denise,

Despite all of my fears and reservations, it seemed as if Tracey and I were destined to meet. I figured if it was supposed to happen, it would happen. The retreat had been held in the summer. The following February, which is Black History Month, my cousin Harold called me. He attended a predominantly Black church called Harvest Community Church. Although I was not a member of that congregation, I had visited a few times and knew many of the members, including the pastor, Mike Jones, very well. That church was very involved with the Emmaus community. Harold called me one day to ask if I was going to speak at the church during Black History Month. His pastor had told his members they were going to have a surprise speaker at that time. Harold assumed it was going to be me, but it wasn't. I suspected something right away.

I called the pastor and asked him point-blank if Tracey was going to be their speaker for Black History Month. He said that she was, and asked me how I knew. I told him I had put two and two together. He said that he would love to have me there too. I told him I had to be honest: I didn't know how I felt about being there with her, even though I knew how I was supposed to feel as a Christian. I needed to think that invitation through. Her father was responsible for the death of my sister. Was I really going to meet her and be nice to her? Or was I going to meet her and show her anger for what her father had done to you? I told the pastor that I needed to check to see if it was okay with my parents. Several weeks later, my cousin asked if I was coming to hear the speaker, and I said I still wasn't sure.

Finally, I called the pastor and I told him I was coming, but I wanted to sit in the audience and hear what she had to say. I didn't want her to know I was coming. I don't think I told Kim I was going. Mamma and Daddy were suffering from Alzheimers and dementia, and despite all the difficulties and sadness that their dementia brought to our lives, one blessing was that I didn't have to share anything about this invitation with them, as it would only upset them.

I called my friend Mindy, who went to the retreat and first told me about Tracey, and told her I was going to hear Tracey speak at this church. She insisted on going with me. She in turn asked another Black friend of ours to come as well, so we all went to the service together. When I arrived, I stopped at the pastor's office to let him know I was there, and he informed me that he thought it would be good if I met Tracey after the service for a meal. I had a photo shoot after church, however, and could not make it. He also wanted to introduce us to each other during the service. I wasn't sure about that, but I agreed.

Church began and, not long into the service, Pastor Mike introduced Tracey. He didn't give much information about who she was, just a brief synopsis. Keep in mind that this was an African American church, so there may have been only two or three white people present. A couple of the members knew who she was.

Tracey got up and told a story of how she grew up with her father who had indeed helped with the bombing. She described him as an angry and hateful man who loathed Black people. Consumed with rage and bitterness, he was hateful toward his own children, depriving Tracey of any semblance of a normal childhood, and she feared for her life because of all the bombings and other violent acts he perpetrated. Tracey's father was one of the men who was never brought to trial.

When Tracey went to school, she had Black classmates. Her family urged her to hate them, to refer to my people by using the "N" word, and to treat those of our race as less than human. For some reason, she could not bring herself to do that, for she knew in her heart that it was wrong. As she got older, her family stopped communicating with her because she would not do as they were doing. Tracey told us about her grandfather, her dad's father, who was a good Christian man. Her grandfather taught her about the love of Christ and how He loves us all, no matter who we are. That made sense to her, and she said if it weren't for him, she wouldn't have known about that kind of love.

As it turns out, she was eventually ostracized from the entire family. When her father died, they didn't include her name in the obituary. She was cut off from any inheritance she was due to receive, and no longer has a relationship with her mother or siblings. Through Christ and the love of her church and Emmaus community, however, she testified that she had a new family with people who love her, love God, and love others. She went on to describe how she overcame all the hatred and anger in which she was raised through Christ's love and by His grace.

It was interesting to watch the posture and demeanor of those in the audience. When she began speaking, I could tell most folks were not sure what to make of her, but that changed as she told her story. Many people present began to quietly weep as she related her life with, and after, her father. After she finished speaking, the audience gave her a rousing applause. The pastor then gave a short sermon about forgiveness and love, tying it in to what Tracey had said. After he spoke, he asked if Tracey and I would come up to the front.

People in that church knew me because I had spoken there before and they were my friends, but this was different. The pastor still wanted Tracey and me to meet in front of the whole congregation. As I said, this made me uneasy. It struck me as unnecessarily sensational and overly dramatic, the kind of encounter you might see on *The Jerry Springer Show*. But I decided that it was something that had to be done, so I stood up and walked to the front of the church.

This is the picture of Tracey Foster and me when we first met after she shared that her father was one of the men who helped plan the bombing that killed you. From left to right: Alicia Grant, me, and Tracey Foster. Photo by Kevin Cunningham.

The pastor asked me to speak first. I told Tracey that I was your sister. Of course, she was more than a little shocked.

I told her through tears that I had met Reverend Billy Kyles, a minister from Memphis who was on the balcony of the Lorraine Motel with Dr. King when he was shot. When he would speak to groups, Reverend Kyles would say that "segregation and racism were *painful* for Black people and *shameful* for white people." He said, "we tend to sweep all that under the rug and don't deal with it. But the only way to let true healing take place is to sweep it out from under the rug and deal with it." I told her I appreciated her taking her shame and pain out from under the rug and dealing with it. We hugged. She was crying, and so was I.

The pastor asked all the women who would have been around your age when you died to come forward, and they all laid hands on us and prayed for Tracey and me. I have a picture of us standing up and praying while the other congregants embraced us. That was how the service ended. It was a beautiful day. Though I was invited to lunch with Tracey after the service, I did not get a chance to go.

Almost a year passed before Tracey and I finally found the time to meet at a local Thai restaurant. I think Tracey was nervous, and I *know* I was. I felt that she and her story were genuine, and there was no racial conspiracy to get me, yet I was still suspicious. Growing up as we did in Alabama, you can understand why I was still a little leery. As I waited for her outside the restaurant, I was thinking, "Oh Lord, the Klan is going to do a drive-by shooting or something." Of course, that was silly, so I prayed God's protection over myself and waited.

She came, we hugged, and we spent about two hours together over dinner. It went very well. She is a very sweet woman who was worried that I would be angry with her and dislike her. Nothing could have been further from the truth. I really had no reason to hate her. She didn't set the bomb, she didn't kill you. Not only was she not there to represent her father's side, she also chose to see that his hate was wrong. I had to respect her for that.

I mentioned my meeting with Tracey to one of my girlfriends who worked with our local NBC TV affiliate. She kept pressing me to let her cover that story, but I told her that Tracey was shy and private about her past. When Tracey shared her story in that retreat, she had never told it to anyone else. None of her friends knew about her dad or his background.

That day when Tracey came to church, she brought a visual display, a time line showing what her father had said publicly about the accusations against him over the years. The more I thought about it, the more I had to agree with my television friend that it was a good, important story about reconciliation and that it needed to be shared. Therefore, I called and asked Tracey if, when Black History Month came up again, she would consent to have someone do a news story about the two of us. Tracey said she'd be happy to do so if it would make me happy, so we agreed to do it.

The show turned out well, and they have actually re-aired the story in subsequent years since it first aired. Now Tracey and I are Facebook friends and we stay in touch. Interestingly enough, Tracey and her family actually took in a foster child who is Black, and later adopted him. There is reconciliation taking place in Alabama, the Heart of Dixie. That is part of Dr. King's dream, too, but most importantly, that is God's desire for us all.

The healing process is strange and mysterious. Someone once likened it to peeling an onion, one layer at a time. Healing, spiritually and emotionally, from your death and the trauma of being Black in Alabama has been a process far more difficult than I would have thought it to be. Meeting Tracey caused some pain, but it also brought some healing for both of us, and that's a good thing.

There were other pains yet to come, and from unexpected places: 16th Street Baptist Church, specifically, the church in which you died. Sadly, it became a community of which we could no longer remain a part, and I can't put off telling you any longer about what happened there.

Much love,
Your Sister Lisa

Church Can Be a Painful Place

Dear Denise,

I have put off talking in detail about my life in the church because it is so painful and embarrassing. We were still members of 16th Street Baptist Church when I was in my late teens. I changed a bit when I became a teenager, as I suppose all teens do. When I was little, I went to church and sat on the front row. As I got older, I no longer wanted to sit on the front row, because Mamma was in the choir and could see everything I was doing.

My friends and I ended up sitting on the side of the church toward the back. Teenagers are goofy, and I was no exception. Mamma could see all over the sanctuary from the choir loft and there was no place to hide. The rest of the kids at least tried to hide in the darkest spots of the sanctuary where they could not be seen, but not me. Even though I sat in the back too, I wanted to sit on the side of the church where the light came in through the beautiful stained-glass windows. Again, I gave Mamma a perfect view of what I was doing, or not doing, and I would hear about it on the ride home.

In my teens, 16th Street's membership started to become fractured as people argued over the church's pastoral leadership. Some of the members didn't like the minister who came after Reverend Cross, who was your minister. The new minister's name was Reverend James T. Crutcher. His son was the one who escorted me to the debutante ball events. The church membership voted him in, but over time people had a strong aversion to the new things he instituted. The changes weren't that big of a deal; in fact I thought they were all pretty cool.

For example, he started a choir for children under twelve. Some people didn't like that. He started a gospel choir, which sang more contemporary music and not just traditional anthems. A lot of people didn't like the upbeat music, but we enjoyed it. It seemed like some people just hated any change on principle, no matter what it was—unless they thought of it themselves. He opened the church to anyone who wanted to come. That didn't sit well with some people, either. Over time, 16th Street had taken on an air of elitism and didn't seem to want folks to join if they were in a lower income bracket. At the time there were many people who fit that description who lived downtown, and our family believed that anyone who wanted to come and learn about Jesus was welcome. To minister to them would have been a great move of God.

Some people didn't like this minister and didn't want him to have a say in church matters. They felt he should only show up to preach on Sunday and visit the sick, and that was it. The majority of us, however, felt he was a good and kind man of God and that he was doing a good job.

His opponents tried to vote him out a number of times, but the overwhelming majority of the members liked him and wanted to keep him. They felt like his pulpit messages were sound, but those folks who resisted change didn't like him no matter what he did or we said. Instead of abiding by what the majority said or just packing their bags and leaving, his enemies actually took him to court to try and get rid of him, which was ridiculous. He wasn't a criminal and had broken no laws. The first time they tried to have him legally removed, the case was thrown out of court.

In the meantime, we would have terrible church conference meetings. There was much animosity between those who wanted to keep our pastor and those who didn't. When I attended a church meeting, I ended up listening to two to three hours of verbal arguments. It was embarrassing and the opposite of how God wants us to treat each other. One crazy lady brought a gun to one of the meetings. It was bad. As a child it was terribly sad to see adults I had been taught to look up to and admire behave so badly.

The strife went on and on, until the year I was preparing to go to college. The church had a tradition of presenting children in the congregation some money for college from a scholarship fund. Mamma was upset because when my time came, they didn't give me any money, since they were angry with her because she liked the minister and was on his side. I felt it was wrong for them to mistreat Mamma because she had lost so much in that church.

Even after his position was renewed by an overwhelming majority, a select few took the pastor back to court to try and oust him. They not only took him to court, but they also sued his supporters, like Mamma, our cousin Mamma Helen, Auntie Nee Nee, and other dear church friends. It was such a sad time. All of it was a hateful, non-Christian, mean-spirited way to behave. It was so embarrassing. Their actions were all over the news, but the court threw the case out again. What happened next you are not going to believe.

One Sunday we came to church and couldn't get in the building. The malcontents had locked us out! I could not believe these people had locked us out of our own church. Reverend Crutcher was a forward-thinking and loving man, and he made the best of this bad situation. He said we were going to have church and praise the Lord anyway, so we had service on the front steps.

The press got wind of the news and those who locked the doors were embarrassed and angered by the coverage. But that didn't stop them. Instead of being nice and opening the door the next week, they got a temporary court order and banned every one of us from gathering on the church property. I don't know how they got it, but we couldn't have church on the steps. Then Reverend Crutcher said we'd have church in Kelly Ingram Park, which as you know is across the street from 16th Street. It was fun. We brought blankets and picnic food, sat on the grass, and had a wonderful time. Later that week the court order was lifted, and we could resume our worship inside the next Sunday.

This type of foolishness had been going on for about ten years, and the abuse and bickering wore on everyone over time. Those opposed to Reverend Crutcher were just as vicious to his wife and children. For example, someone called Stephen while he was away at college and told him his father had died. This was not true, but it was done just to be cruel. There was nothing Christian about how they behaved. It was hard to go to a church that had so much animosity.

On the Sunday after we were allowed back inside, Reverend Crutcher got up in the pulpit and said he really enjoyed the people there and was thankful for the opportunity, but he was going to leave. We were devastated and heartbroken. Reverend Crutcher and his family were such awesome people and his ministry there was doing so many positive things. Many of us began to weep. It broke our hearts to see him leave. What happened next almost closed 16th Street for good, because 80 percent of the church membership left and joined other church fellowships after he was gone. Often you hear of churches splitting up because members leave with the departing minister. That didn't happen here. Those who departed didn't follow him because he didn't have a church where he was preaching. He joined another church as just a member and it was quite a while before he preached at a church again. He didn't split the church, but the heart of the church was gone. We were part of that 80 percent who did not return.

That was traumatic for me because 16th Street was my church family. I had known those folks from birth and, of course, we had a special history there because of the bombing and your murder. Mamma's family had worshiped there for several generations. It was heartbreaking. Kim took it really hard. My heart hurt for her. She would often ask Mamma if we were ever going back to visit there. Her answer would always be "no." When she asked Mamma Helen if she was going back, she would also say "no," and when she pressed her as to why she would say, "not enough people over there have died yet." I guess she was really angry. We didn't know what we were going to do. For my debutante program, I had to list where I went to church, so I put Daddy's church because I didn't want to be connected with 16th Street. I had no allegiance to them any longer, and I didn't want to be associated with a church where people could act in the ways they did. Sadly a few angry, bitter people ruined a good thing for all of us.

This was our church, this was *your* church, and we had such a long history there. It struck me as odd that white folks had treated us so badly for so long, but in this situation, it was our own people who were being so mean *to one another*. I guess no one race has a corner on meanness or sin.

Daddy always used the phrase "human beings" when he talked about folks and what we do, instead of ascribing certain behaviors and flaws only to white people or only to Black people. He understood a long time ago that we are all the same; there is good and bad among all of us.

Where did I finally start to attend church again? You will be shocked when I tell you.

Much love,
Lisa

White Church

Dear Denise,

After we left 16th Street Baptist, we were hurt, and at first, we didn't know what to do. We were not "church-hopping" kinds of people and 16th Street was all we had known, so for a while we just drifted. We stayed home on Sunday and watched church on TV. Mamma Helen, however, had been visiting a predominately Black church by the name of New Hope Baptist Church. She liked it a lot, and not long after we all left 16th Street, she joined there. She always was the one who was on top of things. She probably sensed that 16th Street was not going to get better and had been looking for a new church home for a while. We all knew that no matter what, we had to find one. We could not live in limbo without one for very long. Dear Dear, soon followed her, and then Auntie Nee Nee.

Mamma, Kim, and I took a bit longer to make up our minds. Mamma eventually joined New Hope, as I thought she would. After all, her mother, sister, and first cousin were there, and they were all close, as I'm sure they were when you were alive. For a while, Kim and I didn't attend anywhere regularly. I shopped around and visited other churches, even Daddy's church. Then I started visiting Sardis Baptist, also a predominately African American church. I found it to be an awesome church. Ms. Laura, our hairdresser, was a member of that church. I would imagine she did your hair too. She had been singing the praises of her church for years and had invited us to attend many times.

I became a member there and stayed for almost twenty years, leaving in 2003. It was great, and Kim joined there shortly after I did. The pastor, Reverend Samuel Pettagrue, had a heart for teaching the Word and Christian education. Church services there didn't have a lot of whoopin' and hollerin'. Instead, He taught the Word and was a good preacher. He had a heart to reach men and equip them to lead and minister to their families. The choir was amazing, and I joined it shortly after I became a member. Because of Sardis, my walk with the Lord became stronger. Reverend Crutcher and his family were members there too, and it was good to see them. He had taught me a great deal at 16th Street, but Reverend Pettagrue helped to broaden my faith with his ministry. I learned so much about the Bible and improved my walk with the Lord. We always studied and read passages from the Bible that applied to real life. Reverend Pettagrue always told us to read the Bible for ourselves. He would say, "don't just listen to what I have to say but study and read it for yourself." He was a wise man and understood that man can twist the words of the Bible, but if we read and study it ourselves we can never go wrong. I liked that about him.

They also offered many retreats to help us improve our walk with the Lord. Sardis had a great singles ministry. We partnered with two other churches' singles ministries, which made it even more effective. (I imagine you would have married and not have been single as long as I have been.) Sardis sponsored monthly singles activities, and those helped me understand that being single meant more than waiting around to get married. I learned that I had a purpose to fulfill in my time of singleness. I was to be at peace in my singleness and view it as a blessing and not a curse. Other churches would come to our singles' retreats because they were so good and the speakers were so informative. Sardis would bring in national speakers to lead workshops at these weekend retreats. We learned much to help us avoid the pitfalls of singleness. We also learned that because we were single, we had more time to attend to the work of the Lord. I learned how to stay encouraged while single and not be sad because I wasn't dating and had not married. That was hard sometimes, since during this time in my life so many of my friends were getting engaged and marrying. It felt like being the last one to be chosen for the softball team; I didn't know why I wasn't getting picked and it made me very sad and very unwanted at times. Also, older adults would always ask me "when are you going to get married? Didn't I want to give my parents grandchildren?" I deliberately never ask young people that because it used to really get under my skin and make me feel bad. Because, really, there isn't an answer for that question if you are single and not seriously dating anyone. It's a stupid question because it isn't something I can do on my own. A man would have to ask me to marry him, but before that he would have to ask me to date him in a committed relationship. If that wasn't happening, I didn't understand why people who would ask that question didn't get that it was something that was out of my hands. This was in God's hands. I would often tell them that. That would usually shut them up. All anyone would respond to that comment is, "yes, you are right." But the fellowship with other singles was very uplifting and encouraging.

Sadly, the singles' ministries in churches often have short shelf lives. They tend to be strong for a while, but then they phase out and die. We had some strong singles' leaders, but then they moved on, fell in love, or got married. The church tried to keep their ministry momentum going, but then when the leaders are married, their life emphasis is no longer the same. Over time, our singles department lost its oomph. I was the president of the ministry for two or three years. I was only supposed to serve one term but no one else wanted to take up the mantle.

Pastor Pettagrue was older but he enthusiastically supported the singles ministry. He had many other things to deal with in such a large church. Then the church bought a new and bigger building, and everyone was thinking how wonderful and great we were. We started thinking more about our new large facility and forgetting that Jesus was the main reason for coming to church. It was by His grace that we had enjoyed any success at all. More of that "human being" behavior, I guess. Leadership at the church kind of lost its way, things began to falter, and the ship started to sink.

I went to the Sardis Church conference meetings when things started to decline, which I didn't do for a while because of the bad experience I had with the meetings when I was still at 16th Street. I think I had spiritual PTSD! The first time I went to one at Sardis, I was trembling because the ones at 16th Street had been so volatile. After attending some good ones at Sardis, the meetings started to resemble the ones I had come to hate at 16th Street. Not quite as bad, but the energy was the same.

I knew this one meeting was going to be rough. I brought my Bible and had highlighted some Bible verses that I was prepared to share. When things got tense, I felt led to share some of God's word. It's odd we don't go there first as human beings. I read some passages that spoke to how the people were behaving and pointed out that their behavior wasn't what the Lord desired from His people. I reminded them that the Bible states we aren't dealing with flesh and blood but with wicked principalities and powers of our adversary, the devil. Many members hadn't heard me speak before and were surprised at what I had to say. God's word and the verses I read lifted the spirits of those present. Everyone prayed and resolved some things before the end of the meeting. It was a good feeling. That's how God wants us to work together.

Unfortunately, the peace was short-lived, so I started going to church less and less. I stayed in bed to watch church on television, or I would visit a different church. I was upset about leaving Sardis, because I had already left one church and didn't want to be someone who could not commit and jumped around from church to church. Yet I knew I wasn't getting fed from the Word there any longer, and had to make a change.

One of the broadcasts I would watch on Sunday morning was from a predominantly white church by the name of Dawson Memorial Baptist Church. It was a local church and I always enjoyed their message. It has been said by some that the Sunday morning church hour is one of the most segregated hours of the week in America, and it's true, but getting better. After some time, I joined this church.

I want you to know that I tried to make it work in a Black church. I learned, however, that it is not about the race of those at a church, but whether or not I was growing in God's word, the congregation was loving, and the church was reaching out to meet the needs of the world around them. I joined Dawson in the fall of 2003. When I would watch it on TV, Daddy, who wasn't a big church person at this point in his life, would watch it with me. One Sunday, I saw a young couple that happened to be the first African American couple to join Dawson. They had also been members with me at Sardis. I told them I liked Dawson and often watched it on TV. They invited me to come as their guest.

I had been curious to see what Dawson looked like up close and personal, because it sure looked pretty good on TV. Interestingly enough, I didn't sit with the couple on the Sunday I came to visit. I got the directions confused, entered through the wrong door, and couldn't find them. The sanctuary was very large, with several levels. Later, I saw them in the balcony. That seems to be my way in life. I often go through things all by myself—with God guiding me, of course. I am used to it now.

I had a great experience. Before I could get out of my seat and out the door after the service ended, the minister at the time, Gary Fenton, came quickly down the aisle to shake my hand personally and welcome me. He knew Daddy from Rotary Club. He was kind and sweet, and called me later in the week to thank me for coming, which I thought was special. Dawson is a church with a membership of about 6,000 people, and I thought, "Who there has the time to call anyone?"

I went back a second time months later and he remembered me by name and was once again gracious. Dawson did minister to its single members, but in a very different way than we did at Sardis. At Dawson, along with all of the other Sunday school classes, they had classes just for single individuals. What was unique about them is they were arranged by age groups: twenties to thirties, thirties to forties, forties to fifties, and sixties to seventies. I really liked this because there was a place for any age group to fit in. I started regularly attending a singles class for my age group, and the Sunday school teacher was dynamic. They had a lot of weekly activities, so I had a chance to meet a lot of other singles. I didn't even have to be a member to participate. I really liked that. They also had women's conferences and luncheons and so many other activities that had substance and were also well organized. At one point, Sardis had a lot of different activities, but they had become few and far between.

I had been visiting Dawson more and more, but I was still going to Sardis because I was in the choir. I would sing at Sardis on the first and third Sundays and visit Dawson on the other Sundays. I wanted to join Dawson but I had trepidations. The only reason was that Dawson was a white church. My last name was McNair, Daddy was a well-known, public, African American figure, and I came from a family that had a Civil Rights history. How could I join a church with the white people? What kind of flack was I going to get for that? What were people going to say about giving my tithes over to white people when so many of our people need help? I had all this stuff in my head about why I couldn't go there, but I kept praying and asking for guidance because I wanted to do God's will.

At the end of the day, I decided it's not about what color anyone is. It's about my spiritual walk, how I am being fed, and where God wants me to be at any given time. I prayed and kept waiting for an answer. Sometimes God will tell me things and I instantly know it's His voice. One Sunday I went to church at Dawson, and a lady I knew from Sardis was there. It was great to see her, but I didn't realize she had been attending there for almost as long as I had been going. Because Dawson was so big and had so many services, I had not seen her there before.

As we talked, she was saying the same things I had been saying about why she hadn't joined. Every excuse she gave sounded so shallow coming from her. It was while I was talking to her that I realized that God was answering my question about whether I should join. It became crystal clear that all my excuses were pointless. I also discovered that Dawson had several mission ministries that served lower income areas and were geared to help people of color. That put me over the top. I also found it interesting later that two former Sardis members led me to join Dawson. God truly had a plan in that.

The only thing Dawson didn't have was all the different types of music that my choir sang at Sardis. At Dawson, we sing anthems that were very much like what we sang at Sardis, but there we had also sung more contemporary gospel music. Our music at Sardis had flavor. You could dance to it, and sometimes we did. Sardis's songs had rhythms taken from the sounds of blues, R & B, and jazz. We would have a very spirited, jamming good time praising the Lord. That was one thing I did sacrifice by joining Dawson. Rarely—if ever—do we sing music at Dawson that you can move to. Don't get me wrong—it is very good music. It praises and honors God, but it is not what most African Americans in the country are accustomed to hearing at church.

That next week I called Pastor Fenton and told him I had made up my mind to join Dawson. The next Sunday, I walked down the aisle and he recited a beautiful prayer with me about joining. He called me his sister, and that meant a great deal to me. I have been there ever since. I expected to experience some racism, and I would say I have experienced some, but nothing overt. Gary had worked with the congregation to help them be more open to other races of people. I had seen him preach about that when I watched him on television. There were a few times when walking through the halls that I have made eye contact with others and greeted them, only to get no response at all. But for the most part, it has been a loving and caring congregation. On the fiftieth anniversary of your death, I honored you with a huge, beautiful floral arrangement in the vestibule. Gary, said some beautiful words about you and the other girls during the church service and then offered prayers. It was so nice.

There you have it—my story of joining a white church. In a sense, your death, along with the deaths of other Civil Rights heroes, made it possible for me to be free to go worship wherever I want, wherever God wants me to go. Daddy later in life joined another Lutheran congregation that was predominately white. Times have really changed.

Let's move on; I need to fill you in on my love life. Thank God I have Jesus, because it has been a trip.

Love,
Lisa

Unlucky at Love

Dear Denise,

I guess like any girl I wanted to go out on dates and have a boyfriend. Society kind of demands it. Relatives and family friends ask kids at an early age, "Do you have a boyfriend? Do you have a girlfriend?" To me, it always seemed terribly inappropriate to ask a little kid that. I guess you could call me a romantic. I always wanted a boyfriend and to be married. It seemed like a good thing. I dreamed of all the fun things I could do with a guy—things like go out on dates, hold hands, and have someone to take me to parties and social events, to talk to, and, of course, to kiss. Television and children's stories always matched people up. The prince was always rescuing the damsel in distress and they lived happily ever after. Sadly, real life isn't very much like that. As I have gotten older my desires have shifted to wanting a man to share my life with. I have been on a wonderful journey and I don't want to do it alone. The social scene and dating were more difficult to master than anyone made it out to be, or at least how I imagined it to be. It was especially difficult for me.

Being a part of that first Black generation to integrate was especially difficult when it came to dating. People were still expected to date within their race. White people dated white people and Black people dated Black people, and so on and so forth. To do otherwise was taboo. However, society made that difficult for me because all of the men on TV and in magazines were, for the most part, white. I imagine most girls are attracted to their daddies first as the first man in your life. You pattern whom you like after him. But television actors, movie stars, and musicians also play a role in who we are attracted to. When I was little there were almost no Black men on TV to admire. Racism in television was still very prevalent. Seeing a Black face on TV was a rare occurrence. Now we are everywhere, but back then when a Black person was on TV the whole Black community knew it. We would call each other and say, "there is going to be a Black person on TV tonight on channel 42!" It was really special. As I have already mentioned, there was only one Black, male TV star I remember from my childhood, Greg Morris from *Mission Impossible*. All of the other characters on that show were white. In fact, as hard as I try, I can't recall any other Black men on TV but him. Mr. Morris made a special appearance here in Birmingham and Daddy and Mamma took me to meet him. I was so excited and could hardly wait to meet him. However, when my turn came in line I could hardly speak. I just smiled and felt paralyzed. What was funny is that after the event was over, I told everyone I saw that I met Greg Morris. They didn't know that I didn't say more than two words to him.

The only other celebrities I remember being attracted to were white. My first TV crush was Tom Jones, a musician from the country of Wales. He was really attractive. Like other girls my age I later had a big crush on the character Greg Brady

Television actor Greg Morris and me, when Morris made a public appearance in Birmingham. Photo by Chris McNair.

on the TV show *The Brady Bunch*, and a really big one on Keith Partridge on *The Partridge Family*. There were others but those guys stood out. Sadly, I could like them from afar but it was truly taboo to say so out loud. I remember one time a girl at school asked me who I thought was cute on TV and I said Keith Partridge. She said, "you can't like him, he is white." I quickly responded back, "so because he is white he can't be cute?"

Liking a white guy from television was one thing, but in Alabama you sure could not do so in real life. That was a problem because by that time I was at Advent, where there were almost only white guys, and I liked them. I had crushes on the cute boys in our school just like the other girls in our class did. The only difference is I was Black and they all were white. I had a great deal in common with them and besides, they were there. When I was at Advent I only remember two Black guys my age or older there. One was an upperclassman and the other was in my class but only for one year. But we all knew that interracial dating was completely off the table. No white guy could bring a Black girl home to meet his folks, and vice versa. That being the case, you tried not to even let yourself think about it. It is a whole segment of your life that you have to shut off. It was very sad. I felt I was being punished for something I had no control over.

I didn't fit the mold of most of the other Black girls I knew. I was a cute little girl, but an awkward teen. And being an awkward teen who also went to school with mostly white kids—and the one Black kids teased for "talking white"— didn't help either. Mamma, Auntie Nee Nee, and Mamma Helen dressed me well, but it wasn't what was in style. They didn't know what was in style and neither did I. Then, being a "nice girl" sometimes limits you. Not that I wanted the guys who only wanted to sleep with me, but it kept me from getting dates with others, too—or at least that's how I perceived it. I have had so many nice guy friends over the years say that I intimidated them. What is that about? That's ridiculous. How are we ever going to get together and really know one another if men are scared of rejection? Girls are afraid of rejection too. I basically think that is a lie men tell, because other women are getting dates every day. Some men are pushing past their feelings of intimidation. Dating was difficult to figure out then and even now.

High school was a total bust where dating was concerned, and I ended up only having one date. All that fuss I put up not to go back to ASFA and not to enroll in Altamont, and I still didn't get a date with any guy at my high school. The one date I did have was with a Black guy from a different school who went to 16th

Street Baptist with me—not Stephen Crutcher but another guy who said he had loved me from afar. It's funny, but I never remember ever seeing him at church. Sixteenth Street had a decent-sized congregation, but it wasn't *that* big. I knew practically everyone, and I never remembered seeing him at all. He took me out a couple of times in my junior year of high school. Mamma was *thrilled*, to say the least. He was nice enough, but he was needy and "clingy." He told me once he had our whole life planned out. That was just on the first date. I was thinking, "Really? I am only in the eleventh grade!" I didn't date him long. He was already in his freshman year of college, but he made me quite uncomfortable. I felt bad that I stopped seeing him because I didn't want to hurt or disappoint him, but I just didn't feel about him the way he felt about me.

I thought that college would be better. Surely, among all those students I would meet one nice Black guy with a similar background to mine, or maybe even a white guy who would not be afraid to ask a Black girl out. It was a whole new world. Sadly, it was a bust for me all the way around. I did go out on three dates. One was with a guy who was nice but sort of goofy. I don't mind nerdy and goofy, and I actually liked nerds, but this guy was excited to be dating me because my dad was Chris McNair. He talked about Daddy throughout the entire date. Needless to say, I didn't go out with him again. I wanted someone who wanted to date me for who I am, not because of who my father was.

Another date was with a guy who seemed nice and funny. I went out on a double date with one of my friends and one of his friends, and we had a great time. Afterwards, however, they wanted to go to bed with us. I am not really a prude about those things, but this is *not* the way Mamma raised us. We were supposed to wait until we were married to have sex. Mamma, Auntie Nee Nee, Dear Dear, and Mamma Helen constantly preached that to us—well, at least to me. Years later I asked Kim if she remembered them having the birds and bees talk with her and she said they never did. Things have changed in the world regarding dating from when they were kids but surely those guys didn't think one cheap meal of fried chicken was going to make that happen.

The third guy I dated was from Africa. I was excited to go out with him because I had only met one other person from that continent, and I wanted to learn about the place where our ancestors came from. He was very polite but there was an immediate disconnect between us. He wanted to move the relationship along really fast, kind of like that guy from 16th Street, but I wanted to get to know him better. After the first date, he called me constantly, and that became annoying. I tried to let him down gently but he was not good at taking a hint. I finally had to say, "Stop calling me. I don't want to go out with you anymore," to which he replied, "So you are saying you don't want to see me anymore?" I screamed, "Yes!"

By this time in my life I was obsessed with finding a boyfriend, I wanted to have dates for events, someone to buy me flowers for homecoming, just someone to hang with; a man who wanted to be with me for me. Everybody else had someone, why not me? Sadly, I was flunking out of school while trying to do this and save the world at the same time. I am probably the only person to be sent home on academic suspension for volunteering too much and trying to look good in order to catch a man.

As I stated before, after I was sent home to sit out for a semester, I was devastated. Gerald, the white guy I really liked, was left behind in my transition. This began to weigh heavily on me, and part of me wanted to just give up. The social scene for me was just too painful, but at twenty it was difficult not to want to have love in my life when it was all around me. I wanted to know why I couldn't have what many other girls had. I was a nice girl, I was smart, I was cute, why not me? I did *everything* my parents and God told me to do. Why was it so hard to find a nice guy to like me?

I know there were and are nice men in the world. But why were there so many jerks out there? Why was I still in Alabama, where the possibility of dating a white guy or a guy of another race seemed to be out of the question? I have always thought of moving to another state: California, maybe, or up North or to the East coast. I wanted to be in a state where the pool of people to date would not depend on the color of my skin. Even now, I think I might need to leave here to find love. I also considered Paris, France. I have heard they love our people over there. I remember growing up and learning about the actress Josephine Baker living there and being treated like a regular person. I would love that.

Months after working for a while after I had left Bama, I earned enough money to fly to visit our family in California. It was so cool there. I experienced almost none of the silly racist things that I had in Alabama. Our cousins there interacted with white folks and other people from many different races seamlessly. It was a real melting pot. I loved it!!! I stayed there for about ten days, but I wanted to stay a lifetime. Sometimes I still think I would like to live out there.

Months passed and by this time I was attending UAB. It was an urban campus, not like Bama. Most of the students lived at home or in off-campus apartments, not on campus. It was fun getting to know new people. I was active with Alpha Phi Alpha fraternity and they were the coolest guys on campus. Our cousin Nedric is a member of that fraternity and that connection helped me meet many of those guys. They were all nice, very studious, and good looking. They had something called Alpha Sweethearts, which for lack of a better term were like official cheerleaders for them. We were not like real sweethearts or girlfriends, although some of the girls did date the members. You had to interview to be one and I made the cut, which meant so much to me. It made me feel like my Black peers accepted me and really wanted me to be a part of them. That was a great feeling.

I was good friends with lots of the guys, but that seems to be the case with me. I have lots of guy friends, but for some reason only a couple of them ever asked me out. Some said they were afraid of Daddy. I could understand that, but other girls had fathers that no one seemed to fear. It can be hard to have a parent who is famous. You never had to deal with that aspect of our family. I wonder if he ever would have gotten into politics if you had not been killed. Who knows the real answer? Anyway, I had a good time at UAB. By this time, my friend Wendy had graduated from Tuskegee University, having finished in three years. She was quite smart and would often go to the Alpha parties with me. There she met a really nice Alpha whose name was Spencer Horn. He was very smart, well-raised, and a perfect gentleman. They are still married to this day, and they are one of the strongest couples I know.

While at UAB one day, I noticed Barry, a guy I knew from Bama who was a friend of my friend Jennifer. When we would go to a certain nightclub in Tuscaloosa, he would always be there. He was your typical gentleman, another really nice guy, and we had similar backgrounds. He would always buy us drinks and never wanted anything in return. He would dance with us, was a great conversationalist, and was liked by everyone. When we left the club, he would always walk us to our car. I thought that this was the type of guy I wanted to date. He was the kind of man Mamma had told me to look for but the kind who never asked me out. He was a couple of years older than I was, so I thought maybe that was the reason he wasn't interested. In your twenties, a year or two makes a difference. The older you get, the less that matters.

When I saw Barry on UAB's campus, I was surprised. I greeted him and asked how he happened to be in town. He replied that he was going to school and interning in Birmingham. I remembered how nice he was, so I told him to call me if he wanted to know where things were since he wasn't from Birmingham. I didn't know what his dating status was, but I figured that he had my phone number and if he was free and interested, he could call me. We exchanged numbers and went on our way, but I was excited. I hoped that he would call, and he did. We had a great conversation and shortly thereafter, we started to date. I thought "Wow! God finally heard my prayer." We would go to dinner, movies, and even to church (at this time I was going to Sardis). He made dinner for me at his apartment. He would come to my parent's house just to sofa-sit. He and Mamma hit it off right away. He even called her "Mother dear." I thought I had died and gone to heaven. Things were working out just as I had hoped. After all those duds, finally a nice guy and he was Black. That was important because he understood me. I didn't have to try to act "more Black" with him because he was familiar with the way I spoke and the things I talked about. I could be me around him because he too had grown up with a lot of white culture. It was very easy being with him. I think that is how good relationships are supposed to be. Sardis was popular and many of my other male friends from Bama who were in Birmingham for their internships also attended that church. It was a great time in my life.

Months passed and I had not yet told my friend Jennifer that I was seeing Barry. Between work, school, and dating, I didn't have much time to chat with friends or drive down to Tuscaloosa and hang with the gang. Finally, I called her one day from work. After the usual pleasantries, I said "Hey girl, guess who I am dating?" She asked who, and I said, "That really nice guy we would see at the bar, Barry."

The next words out of her mouth nearly knocked me on the floor. She said, "Oh so he isn't engaged anymore?" I was stunned and couldn't believe it. How did I not see that? Why didn't someone say something to me? We were all over Birmingham, so what we were doing was not a secret. He never tried to hide the fact that we went out. We hung out with friends from Bama all the time. And his fiancée also went to Bama.

I didn't know what to do, and then I felt bad for his fiancée. How could he do that to her? As a woman I would never want to do that to another woman. And how could he do that to me? It was awful. There I was, having waited so long for the right guy. He had all the right stuff, and now that news. I had even come dangerously close to breaking Mamma's cardinal rule against having sex before marriage. I felt comfortable with him and trusted him, but I guess that was one circumstance that pointed to the wisdom in her rule.

I didn't know what to do. I told my friend Wendy and she was livid. She thought I should dump him, and so did I. Mamma felt the same, but she was really hurt for me. She also thought he was the one. She was in the store one day and had bought some coffee cups for our future house that Barry and I had not even thought about. I thought that was sweet but a little premature. Daddy was disappointed but his response was very different. He told me I should talk with Barry about it and keep seeing him; "after all, he isn't married yet". I wasn't sure Daddy's idea was right. I wanted to slap Barry and drop him like a hot rock. But Daddy's advice gave me hope to at least wait until I had talked to him because, after all, I did enjoy his company and I had not heard his side. Daddy was male and I thought maybe he knew something about men that I didn't know.

A day or so passed before Barry and I saw each other. I asked him point-blank if he was engaged. He responded, "A little." I responded by saying, "That's like being a little pregnant. You either are or you aren't." He tried to dance around it, telling me they were having problems. Radio personality Dr. Laura would always say that a couple was not really engaged without a ring and a wedding date. I should have asked him if he had either. I didn't, and kept on seeing him, but it was never the same. Wendy was mad at both of us and said if we got married, she would not come to the wedding. I don't think she really meant that, but I could respect her righteous anger.

However, I could not get his fiancée out of my mind. I felt bad that I was seeing her guy. I knew that I would not have wanted anyone to do that to me. I figured out why he was able to see me with so much freedom. His fiancée lived four hours away from Birmingham and the chance of her seeing us together was slim to none. Later, I would really be angry about how I had been deceived. It was close to Thanksgiving, and I heard from my friend Jennifer that Barry's fiancée had a big spread in the Tuscaloosa newspaper announcing the engagement. It was November and they were going to be married in February.

That was the last straw. He would have just married her and kept seeing me! I had to put an end to it. I told him it wasn't right and not fair to his fiancée or to me. He was very upset and even cried. I thought, "Really, man?" I told him he could have been a man and chosen between the two of us, but he didn't, so I had to do the right thing. He still would call from time to time. He wanted me to meet his mother. I thought that was stupid: he was engaged, so why should I meet his mother? I told him "no." A few weeks later I was in Tuscaloosa visiting friends and he got word I was in town. He tracked me down and dragged me to meet his mother. She was very nice and they had a lovely home. On the way back to my car he confessed that she told him to leave me alone if he wasn't going to do right by me. I told him his mother was a wise woman and she was absolutely right. That was the last time I saw him before he got married.

Interestingly enough, and as much as I liked him and enjoyed his company, I never cried about the breakup. I was disappointed and angry, but somehow not sad. I knew I was doing the right thing. He called sometime later and apologized. He did marry the girl and they stayed married until his untimely death. I would see him around town and wonder why he did what he did. We remained cordial but it was very disappointing to have been deceived in that way. I consider myself to be a pretty smart woman. I think of myself as someone who is not going to fall for any old line that men have. Most of them really sound super-stupid and are a complete turn off. But if I could be duped by somebody that easily, it made me wonder about the next guy with whom I would come in contact. It was so disheartening. Men are a trip.

Peace,
Lisa

I Was the Wrong Color

Dear Denise,

My love life is like a desert. There have been long dry spells, then a monsoon, then the desert again. I have mostly dated Black men, although I tended to have more in common with white guys because I was around them so much and we would have similar upbringings. It is not so much the white guy I am attracted to, but more of the lifestyle and the culture. The guys that I have dated and really enjoyed spending time with shared very similar backgrounds and upbringings. Living in the South has really made dating a white guy difficult, because it was taboo for a white guy to date a Black girl and there was no way would they acknowledge it in public. Stupid racism. However, there was one time that I came really close.

As I told you, I worked for years at the Greater Birmingham Convention and Visitors Bureau. After I was told to sit out a year from Bama, I got a full-time job at the bureau. At first, I was in the main office downtown. The bureau, however, was starting satellite offices called Visitor Information Centers. I was asked to head up the one at the Birmingham Race Course. That was during the time I dated Barry. That location didn't work for the bureau just like Barry didn't work for me. I ended up back at the main office.

Later, they opened one at the Birmingham airport. That was a great idea. Lots of visitors traveled in and out of the airport and needed information on Birmingham. Now that was an awesome job! They made me manager and I had one full-time staff person and several part-time staffers. I had never had that level of responsibility before, but I did a really good job and took it quite seriously. I even wrote an operations manual for how things should be run there. At that time, we didn't have a computer at that location, so I would write notes, go downtown to the main office a couple of hours before my shift started every day, and type up the manual. It took several months. I really enjoyed the project and my supervisors were impressed that I had taken such a vested interest in my job. These were good times for me and boosted my self-esteem and self-confidence considerably.

One of the responsibilities I had there, as part of our agreement with the airport, was to maintain the plane ticket pick-up service that then operated from our counter. People from various travel agencies would come by and leave tickets there for clients to pick up, mostly for early-morning flights. Therefore, our counter opened at 5:00 a.m. every day. That is where Danny entered the picture and my life.

Danny was a guy who delivered tickets for one of our local travel agencies. He and I were around the same age. He was tall (though my friend Audra says I don't know what tall is, since I am only 5'4". She says to me, everyone is tall) and had red hair. He was white. He still had a few acne blemishes, and he reminded me of a grown-up Opie from Mayberry. He was working and going to school like I was, so we had a lot to talk about. He had a great sense of humor, which is a trait I really love in a man. I loved it when Danny would come by to drop off tickets.

After a while I noticed he would make our booth his last stop so that he could stay and talk longer, and we would laugh and talk for almost an hour. It was great. We eventually exchanged numbers and began to talk on the phone. He attended church with one of my coworkers from the main office. When I would see her, we would both talk about how we had seen him and the funny things he had said. She was older than both of us and was married.

Eventually, we had lunch outside of work. It was great, and went on for well over an hour. I was so excited because I felt like this might be leading to something other than friendship. A man can get a certain look in his eyes to let you know he likes you, and it's deeper than friendship. Danny had that when he looked at me. I didn't want to make the first move; things were moving slowly but steadily. It was nice.

Soon after that, I had to go to our main office. I saw our mutual friend who attended Danny's church. She said that she had seen him at church, and that he talked about how much he enjoyed spending time with me. Then she said the following, which I will never forget, "He said he likes you a lot but just hates that you are the wrong color." It was just like in the movies. I don't know what she said next. All I could hear was "the wrong color" again and again in my head. It was devastating. I played it off so she wouldn't know how upset I was and quickly made my exit.

I really liked Danny, and obviously I wasn't wrong about him liking me. I knew we were of different races, but this was in the early 1990s. Things were starting to change in this country. I was willing to work with our racial differences. It didn't matter to me. Years earlier I had asked Daddy if he minded if I dated someone who wasn't Black, and he was cool with it.

Danny's words really hurt. I had dated Barry, who seemed nice but was a liar, and now Danny, who would not date me because of my race. I wanted to cry but I didn't dare. I did cry later when no one was around, which is mostly when I cry. I wanted to work this thing out in my head all by myself. I am not sure if I told anyone. When I think about it, who could I have told?

The next time I saw him, it was very different. He was very polite, but something was missing. I knew it was over. He didn't stay long and talk like he had previously. He later talked to me about dating someone, and I wished him well. I lost touch with him. I do sometimes wonder what would have happened if I had confronted him about how he felt toward me? Or if we had tried to have a relationship? We will never know. It was a sad time, and once again I found myself back in the desert without anyone to date.

From that point on I have almost only dated Black men. I have gone out with one or two men who were not Black, but that is all. The older you get, the harder it is to find someone to date. The pool of candidates grows increasingly smaller. Most people are already matched up or they are focused on their careers, or they have been hurt so much they just shut down completely. I have had that experience too. I met a nice guy, but he was hurt so bad that he is married to his work and not really open to a relationship—but I can tell he really likes me. I hate that, because even though I have dated some real stinkers I want a committed relationship with someone who wants one too and wants to be with me. I shut myself off too for a while, so I know what that looks like. I threw myself into my work. But that never lasts. Human beings are supposed to be together. We need each other. Just because it didn't work out with one person, or a second or third person, we should not give up. I still have hope.

Thanks for letting me bend your ear about this topic. I know you didn't live long enough to go out on a date. But if you had lived it would have been awesome to have you to talk about it with. It would have meant so much. Maybe my journey would not have been as bad. I have always envisioned that you would have been popular with the guys and could have had your pick of them.

Love you, my sister,
Lisa

Getting Along

Dear Denise,

I suppose it's not so strange that I ended up at a white church. I have told you about my affinity for white culture that started in elementary school. It was a new world in the South, and there were many more opportunities for our people than when you were alive. There was another factor that affected my preferences and decisions: Mamma and Daddy taught us that we had to love all people, including white folks. I never forgot them telling us that.

If we could talk today, among the first questions I would ask you is: What kind of people were Mamma and Daddy when you were alive? Were they happy? Did they seem to have a good relationship as a couple? What were they like? The people I knew were great, loving parents. They were happy for a while, but for the most part their marriage was not happy. There was a lot of fussing, arguing, and intense discussions, and I wonder how it was with you. Since you were so young when you left this world, you may not have paid that much attention. I like to think they were happy once.

Mamma continued to teach after your passing, and worked for thirty-three years all together. She always loved children and teaching. I have never met anyone who really cared more about their work as a teacher than Mamma. She went above and beyond for her students. I would see her go to students' homes and meet with their parents. She would often take clothes and other things to her students who were in need.

I regularly run into people whom Mamma taught, and they say they wouldn't be the people they are if it wasn't for her. When I hear that from people, it makes me proud of the impact that our Mamma had on this world. When she leaves to join you in heaven one day, part of her will remain here in a lot of people. Students often say what a beautiful woman she is, and that's nice to hear.

By the way, I met a woman not long ago who said she was a student in Mamma's class the year you were killed, and she remembers how sad Mamma was. Your death affected Mamma and Daddy as parents and shaped how they related to Kim and me. They were probably more protective of us because of your death, but it was never articulated. They never said to us outright, "Don't go there or do that because we could not bear to lose another child." While they never said it, we sort of knew that's what they were thinking. Yet, some of it also came from the fact that *all* Black parents had to be protective of their children because our world in Alabama was so dangerous. They told us we could not do certain things because it would only lead to trouble.

As Black people, we had to be careful not only because we could get arrested but also possibly be killed, as our family knew all too well. There were so many things we couldn't do because we were Black. Recently, I was in a store with my friend Mindy, who is white. While in the store we saw some candy that looked really delicious. We felt we had to buy it, so we put it in our shopping cart. While in the checkout line, Mindy was anxious to try it and said, "why don't we open it up and eat some now." I thought she was kidding at first, so I told her no and just laughed it off. She insisted that it was ok to do so because we were going to pay for it. So while we were in the checkout line she opened the box and began to eat it. I was shocked. She offered me some and I told her "no way." I looked at her as if she was crazy! I told her that she was wrong for doing that. She said it was no big deal. I explained to her that Black folks could never do anything like that when I was growing up or we would have gotten in trouble, maybe even arrested. When she informed me that her mother would let her do it when she was a little girl, I told her it was because she's white, but that didn't fly for Black folks. I told her that there was something called "white privilege" that meant she could do something like that and think it was okay, but that was only possible because she was white. That shocked her. She had never thought of it like that or heard the term "white privilege."

That is an example of one of those things Mamma and Daddy would not let us do. It was an example of the privilege that white people enjoyed in this country, and how cautious we had to be not to step out of line or rile up the white establishment. The truth is that no one should open and start eating food before you pay for it in the store but because of white privilege they can do these things and no one will accuse them of trying to steal an item. They get a pass just because of the color of their skin. Mindy had no idea that what she did was not an option for me or any other Black kid. I know it really made her think.

Mamma was around more than Daddy when I was growing up because he worked in his own business and in the legislature a lot. That left Mamma to be the one to whom we addressed most of our questions and the one who informed most of our moral compass. As a child, she warned me that I was Black and that not all white people liked Black people, which was why I couldn't do certain things. We had other conversations like that. I picked up bits and pieces of how I was to act (or not act) as I listened to grownups talk. She also told us that we have to work twice as hard as white folks do in order to get just a small portion of the opportunities they have.

I have already told you that while I was in elementary school, I once asked Mamma if I was supposed to hate white people. Mamma told me, "We have to love all people like Christ loves us. Everyone has a duty to love and we must take each person individually and love them for who they are." That made sense to me as a child.

There was a white woman named Liv May here in Birmingham who appeared as a host every year on the local Jerry Lewis MS telethon. Dear Dear would always say she couldn't stand her; but one year, to my surprise, she told me that Liv was our distant relative. That indicated to me that some of our relatives were white people. That made sense to me because Dear Dear's mother was light skinned and Dear Dear was fair skinned, but not that fair. Our great-great grandmother Mary Jane Cain had a bunch of brothers and sisters, and some of them were so fair that they moved up North and passed for white. I would love to research that side of our family and find out what happened to those folks.

When Dear Dear came down with Alzheimer's, she came to live with us from time to time. Kim came home one time with a bunch of friends and one of them was white. In our kitchen is a big island, and her friend was standing by the island closest to the refrigerator. Dear Dear acted like she was getting something out of the refrigerator, and while Kim's friend's back was to it, she warned, "Watch that one." I was thinking, "Tell me she didn't just do that." Everyone else thought it was funny, but Kim and I were thoroughly embarrassed.

I was also aware of the fact that I was the odd woman out for treating white people with kindness. Sometimes I've been made to feel bad if I entered a room and didn't first sit with the Black people, instead choosing to talk to a white person. I know so many white folks (frankly, folks *period*) in this city that I can rarely go anywhere and not see people I know. Once when I worked for Hand in Paw, we marched in the Veteran's Day Parade. The staff started a game to see just how many people I would know on the parade route. Sometimes I do chat with the

Black folks, but sometimes I deliberately do not just sit with only Black folks, particularly if I go into a room and see white people and Black people who have separated themselves. I want to mix it up. Now you see how I was made aware of the fact that some Black people didn't like white people—and didn't like me liking them, either.

Mamma told me to love all people including white people, but Daddy showed me how to do it. I have told you that he and Mamma refused to go into a shell or retreat into their pain after you were killed. Mamma continued to teach and Daddy went into politics, and had a distinguished career up to the very end, when he got into some difficulties. Let me tell you more about what Daddy taught me that influenced my life and how I relate to white people.

Much Love,
Lisa

What Does It Mean to Be Called a White Girl?

Dear Denise,

This will be a long and important letter about something I have not shared with many people in my personal life. I have mentioned again and again in these letters that sometimes people called me a "white girl" or would say I was "acting white." I wasn't sure you would know what I meant by that, so I wanted to try to explain. I think it will be important to explain why someone would say that to me and I want to make sure you understand. For that matter, I'm still trying to explain it to myself, because it baffled me then and still does to this day.

The first time someone told me I was acting "white," I was confused as to why they would say something that was so obviously untrue, but I did not give it much more thought. The next time it happened, I was angry and offended. I thought, "How can you look at me and not see that I am Black? What's more, my sister, my own flesh and blood, was killed in one of the most heinous crimes in Civil Rights history!" As far as I was concerned, that incident alone cemented my status as an African American person. Who could be more Black than I? I was always talking about Dr. King and sharing with other people the heritage of our people. When it came to Black topics, I could come across as a bit militant.

Eventually I figured out what they meant. People called me "white" because I grew up around a great deal of white culture. As I have explained, I was a part of the first generation of African Americans that didn't live under slavery or the oppression of segregation. By the time I came into a greater awareness of society and how things were and had been, most of that stuff was illegal and had disappeared, in large part, from daily life. There certainly were expressions of it still around but for the most part, I didn't have to encounter it like you did—and as a child, I thought that's how things had always been.

I have only seen pictures or replicas in museums of "White Only" and "Colored Only" water fountains. I bet you could never imagine life without those types of signs, which were part of your everyday life. Daddy told me the story of when he had to tell you that you could not eat at a lunch counter downtown because you were Black. Telling you that broke his heart. That is probably why when we were kids, he would never take us to a fast food place to eat. He and Mamma both would say "we have food at home," although Mamma did break that rule on special occasions when it was just the three of us (Kim, Mamma, and me). Also, Daddy tends to be a bit cheap! Ha Ha Ha.

Kim and I were raised very differently than you were. The only white folks you would have known would have been Pastor Ellwanger and his family from Daddy's church, but we were close with lots of white folks, and we were able to freely interact with them socially. We went to school at Advent where it was 95 percent white, and that became my norm, not knowing that it was a new normal for people like me. We were at school with white folks every day, and they were not just our classmates but became friends. We were treated as equals.

They could not help but create a white culture at Advent, because all of the teachers were white as well as the principal, chaplains, and the librarian. Don't get me wrong, Advent was not oppressive, and that was the shocking part of it. I had anticipated some resistance when I was told we would have to attend school there. I thought we would be harassed and treated badly, but nothing of the kind ever happened. Things at Advent were just the opposite. We were treated well by all the staff—including the principal, whose name was Una Battles. She was very kind and I liked her very much.

But subtly and without knowing it, I was immersed in the white culture around me. There were ways that white people said things that Kim and I started to hear every day, so naturally we began to talk like that without even thinking about it. There were subtle differences in clothing that made us stand out when we were around other Black folks.

The fact that we went to private school in the first place made us different be-cause all of the kids in our neighborhood went to the local public school. Many didn't even know what private schools were, or if they did, they only knew about Catholic schools, where tuition was considerably less expensive than Advent. That right there set us apart from other kids. I have already explained that some people thought we were rich because our parents could afford to pay for us to go to pri-vate school. That was an assumption we have not been able to correct even today.

You remember how Mamma and Daddy lived when you were a child; they didn't have a lot of money. Paying for our private school education was a hardship for our family. Mamma and Daddy went without a lot to make that sacrifice for us. Some folks assumed that we thought we were better than them because of it, but I want to be clear, we *never* intended for anyone to feel that way. Mamma made sure we didn't think of ourselves as better than others and that we didn't have an air of superiority about us. She actually threatened to spank us if we did. She said that would be very wrong if we thought like that.

Also, being at Advent offered us so many different opportunities that many of our neighbors, family, and friends did not have. After your death, many more opportunities opened up for people of color and our parents made sure we took advantage of all of them. We took ballet lessons, attended operas and plays, and went on field trips to all types of places. Because Daddy was a politician in the area, we were allowed to go into the homes of affluent white people and were able to travel to our state capital and see the legislature in session. It was a wonderful way to grow up, and I am sorry you missed out on that.

The fact that we lived very differently from some other Black people never dawned on me until it was pointed out to me. It was only when talking to my friend Lane Reynolds that I realized how different my school experience was. You probably knew her older brothers and sisters; they lived down the street from us. Lane was near my age and I remember begging her mother to let her go to my school because I wanted to go to school with my friend. I guess I was in about the third or fourth grade. I had no idea there was a cost to go to my school, and it was not possible for her family to send her there because her family was large. As a child you just don't understand such things.

Now that I look back, I see that all those differences really did make us stand out. Even our other family members couldn't relate to us. Our closest cousins, Nedric and Lynn, went to public school. They loved us but we were so very different from them. I didn't fit in with them and they knew no one else who was doing things we were doing. They concluded that I was a bit weird because of the things I did in school, like learning to speak French.

As I entered puberty, things became even more difficult. By that time, I had spent many years around mostly white people and had assimilated a lot of white culture. Although I went to church with Black kids, I only saw them at church and one day a week at choir practice. Advent gave us a magnificent education, but it left very little time for fun. As I have already mentioned, we almost never saw the other kids in the neighborhood by the time we got home because there were no longer outside playing but had gone inside to have their dinner and do homework. We mostly saw them on the weekends. For Kim, this worked out well, but not as much for me. I was awkward and had very little interaction with kids my age in the neighborhood. There were only two girls my age: Lane was one and Lynn Williams was the other. I have already told you about Lynn: she was the one whose father was a bishop in the church they attended, and they traveled a great deal. Lynn was almost never home, so she had no time to play with the other kids in the neighborhood. There were several boys in the neighborhood who were my age, but I didn't play much with them. Our across-the-street neighbor Ron and I would occasionally ride our rollers skates together, but that didn't happen often. Mostly I liked to play with the dogs, talk to my friends from school on the phone, watch TV, or read the *World Book Encyclopedia* our grandmother Dear Dear gave us.

The four years between me and Kim made a big difference. While there were only two Black kids near my age at Advent, there were six in her age group. That made the transition for her much better because she had a support group that I didn't have. Also, for some reason, there were many more kids her age in our neighborhood. She had a lot of kids to play and share with. She was much more in tune with her Black experience than I was for many years. Her experience of being called "white girl" didn't come until high school when we were at a public high school, and it really upset her. I was used to it because people had said that to me for most of my life.

I told you already that being called white girl hurt my feelings for a number of reasons. First is that it simply wasn't true. Second, I felt that often people said it to be mean; they used it as a derogatory term based on their fear and lack of understanding of my experiences and not having a label to identify what I was like. After all, they had never seen anyone like me before. I was an unwilling pioneer, since very few Black people in the South were having the experiences I was having. The only other people to do some of the things I was doing were white folks.

Also, it hurt because being accused of "acting white" implied that I was trying to be like or act like the folks that had oppressed us for so long; it meant I was a traitor to my race. That was the last thing I wanted to be known for. I even remember hearing Mamma Helen, Nee Nee, Dear Dear, and Mamma referred to people or even children they knew who happened to be immersed in white culture as sellouts; they would say, "They think they are white." That meant they thought they were better than other Black people. Who knows if that was true? I imagine that came from back in the times of slavery when the slaves who lived in the slave owner's house were often seen to live better than the ones in the field—and sometimes they considered themselves superior! Often, those slaves were children of the slave owner and a slave and had lighter skin than the field slaves. That set up lots of animosity among the slaves. I guess no one wants to see someone get something they don't have without them having an opportunity to get the same thing.

The embarrassing thing about being called "white" is that, sadly, I often wished that I was, which I could never admit to anyone. Most of my white friends treated me well. Nothing was wrong with who I was to them and they loved me as I was. There was no criticism or awkwardness around them; I could be my true and authentic self. Attending Advent had caused this. It allowed me to learn and be comfortable in white culture but drew me away from my Blackness ever so slightly over a period of years. Being with other Black kids my age was so painfully uncomfortable because I just didn't seem to fit in no matter how I tried. It was like I entered a foreign land of which I had only limited knowledge. On top of that, the criticism from my people hurt so much because of our history with white people. For most of our existence in this country, white people treated Black folks like their enemy; we certainly had personal experience with that in our own family. Despite that, I had learned to love my "enemy," and they were good to me. It made me sad that I had earned white people's trust and love, but Black folks—the people I thought were supposed to love me without question—were sometimes so dismissive. No one reached out with the desire to find understanding, and I was miserable.

I was ashamed to find myself liking and identifying with the enemy of my people. For years, I was torn and conflicted because even though my white friends loved me, many of them didn't want me to be *too* Black. They would often say things like "You aren't really Black" or "We like you because you aren't like those other Black people." That made being called a white girl even worse because sometimes, to be liked by my white friends, I had to tone down some of the Blackness that was in me. In some ways, Mamma Helen, Nee Nee, Dear Dear, and Mamma were right about those Black folks being traitors; and here I was one of them. I was at war with who I was, and didn't know how to resolve it or who I could talk to about it.

African American people who called me "white" were uncomfortable with the changes that were occurring in our society. Those changes were what we wanted, what the movement stood for—that we could live together as equals in every area of life. What we didn't know, Black or white, is what that would look and feel like. Logic would dictate that if we, Black folks and white folks lived, worked, and socialized together, we would pick up each other's traits, mannerisms, and other cultural habits. I personally think it's great when that happens.

I have already related to you that often when I share my story, people who are of mixed race (who have one Black parent and one white one) tell me that they can really relate—even though both of my parents are Black. But what really breaks my heart is when a young Black woman comes up to me after one of my speeches and says that she has been called "white girl" and that she doesn't fit in and has had no one to talk to about it. I usually cry with her. I cry for two reasons. One is that I feel her pain because I have walked that walk. Secondly, I am angered that so many years later others are still feeling that pain. I usually give those women my phone number and tell them they can always reach out to me. I didn't have anyone like that to help me and I really wish I did.

Human beings can be so cruel to one another, but the rejection I felt has stayed with me even until today because there *is* a white girl inside of me. I cannot dispute that and am comfortable with her. It is part of what makes me who I am and gives me a wonderful perspective on life. I can integrate myself in lots of settings with a wide variety of people.

But make no mistake: I will forever be Black. No one can ever take that history or experience from me. All Black folks aren't alike. No one can paint us all with a wide brush. I used to feel bad that I didn't fit in for so long and acted and sounded more white than Black, but God doesn't make mistakes. I am very comfortable in my skin now and love both sides of me. Both sides of me help me every day. They have made me a much better communicator with a perspective on both sides—Black and white—and it allows me to be a peacemaker in a lot of situations. I wouldn't change a thing, but it took me a long time to get to that place.

There, I feel better now that I have that off my chest. Now, let me tell you more about our family and our lives after you were gone.

Love you,
Your *Black* Sister, Lisa

Serving All the People

Dear Denise,

After you were gone, Daddy got involved in politics, which I always thought was pretty cool. His only child (at the time) had been murdered by the Klan and he became a public servant who served *all* the people, and I consider that to have been a noble thing to do. As I have told you, he became a legislator and served several terms, and later he was elected to several terms as a county commissioner. I have a picture of him being sworn in as the first African American legislator from Jefferson County. That was a special day. What Mamma and Daddy did after your death was also quite special. They could have been mean, bitter, and hateful, but they were determined to make something positive out of their tragedy.

On this day Daddy was sworn into the Alabama State Legislature. From left to right: Mamma, Daddy, Kim, Mrs. Lugenia Fair (our babysitter), and me. I love this picture. We all look great, especially Mamma in those cat-eye glasses. Photo from the Chris McNair Archives.

This is Daddy being sworn into the Alabama State Legislature in 1973, along with other representatives from Jefferson County. Daddy was the first African American elected to the legislature from Jefferson County. Photo from the Chris McNair Archives.

Daddy was loved as a politician by all people, Black as well as white. That included the blue-collar worker down the street as well as the wealthy white man who lived over the mountain, along with the educated professional Black person. Daddy loved people and they loved him. Mamma says I am like him in a lot of ways in that we just love people.

I like meeting and getting to know new people to find out what makes them tick. That's what Daddy did in the legislature. It was also Daddy's way of standing up to the establishment and saying, "I am not going to retreat or bow down, but go on to build my life and to serve the people, *all* the people. I will serve Black and white people, do a good job, and not succumb to hateful behavior."

Denise, people would call him at home all the time. He never changed our home phone number or had it unlisted after he became an elected official. People would call him to report that their sewage was messed up or some other problem. He would instruct them to call him at the office the next day and he would take care of it. That's what he was like. People knew they could reach out to him. He ran for the legislature a number of times, and one of the areas in his district was Midfield, which (as I've already explained) is the area near our house that, according to Mamma, was the last area to desegregate. The people in Midfield loved Daddy, and it wasn't fake. He would win those districts again and again with no problem.

Daddy actually ran for the US Congress once but didn't win. We were hoping he would have been the first African American congressman from the state of Alabama. Then he ran for US Senate one time and had a good chance of getting in. He got into the Democratic primary and was in a runoff with the incumbent, a white man. By this time, Black people had started to get political power in the state, and there were two Black political machines that controlled things. One was in Montgomery and one was in Birmingham. They were the Alabama New South Coalition and the Alabama Democratic Conference.

The one in Birmingham was run by the first Black mayor of Birmingham, Richard Arrington Jr. The other was run by Daddy's fellow legislator Joe Reed. Daddy wanted to run for the Senate, and didn't think he had to ask anyone for permission to do so (other than our mother). He decided to run but didn't go through the mayor and his political machine, nor did he ask the machine in Montgomery for permission to run. Therefore, both groups were upset with him and did not give him an outright endorsement, even though he was the only Black candidate qualified to do the job and the only one in the race. Politics is such a dirty game.

Those machines were so powerful that they were able to tell people how to vote and they would comply. Because they were mad at Daddy, they didn't want to endorse him. At the same time, they knew they couldn't only endorse the white man, so they issued a *dual endorsement* between both candidates, which split the Black vote. Then the white candidate got the majority of white votes and Daddy only got some of the Black votes. Polls had shown that before the dual endorsement, Daddy had had a great chance to win because he had good following among white voters and, if these machines had done what they should have done, he would have carried most of the Black votes. They did a terrible thing to him and it broke his heart that he came so close to being a US senator. It was also not a good thing for the state, in my opinion.

Not only was that a terrible thing to do to Daddy, but the Democratic Party institutions in Alabama, both white and Black, really shot themselves in the foot by co-endorsing the other candidate—because after that election he then switched parties to become a Republican. It was also bad for Black folks. We could have made history and had a voice in Washington, DC. As I write this, that white man who won is still our senator, and no Black Alabamian has ever won that seat or even been in a position to win it like Daddy was. I sure hope they feel bad about what they did. I was angry afterwards because those guys would call and want to chit chat with Daddy before that election. They called themselves friends. After the election, when they called and I got to the phone first, I would say he wasn't home or was busy. I even told one of them I couldn't believe he had the nerve to call Daddy after what he had done.

Politics opened many doors for us, but it is also full of land mines and traps, and Daddy stepped in one of them. Let me tell you about that now.

Love you lots,
Lisa

Daddy's Dilemma

Dear Denise,

Not only would I like to have had the chance to hear more from you about our parents' relationship, I specifically would have liked to find out what Daddy was like when you were with him. Daddy's a complex person. He's also a person from a generation when men didn't talk much or share information about themselves. Most Black men tended to be stoic since they were often treated as less than men. That must have been difficult and helped shape who he is.

As I mentioned, Daddy grew up in a small, one-horse town in Arkansas. He moved away, went to college at Tuskegee, lived in the big city, was trying to make a living, and then this crisis in his life made his family known throughout the world. When you were killed, he couldn't really do much about it as a Black man. In 1963, he could not talk about it, insist on an inquiry or investigation, or express his outrage, at least not openly. He could not blame it on the system or the lack of police protection. After your death, Daddy moved on to become someone respected and revered in the community, even among the people who were probably responsible for you being killed.

Daddy served many years in the community and did it with such grace and distinction! Unfortunately, he got indicted for bribery after he served as a county commissioner. He was in his eighties at the time. Between you and me, I don't really think he bribed anyone. I think that's the wrong term to use for what happened. What happened was deeper and more complicated than that. The people who were indicted with him were not criminals any more than Daddy was. Did he make some bad choices? Definitely! Did the people in partnership with him make some bad choices? Yes, but I don't think they did anything criminal. Of course, there are some who would disagree. I feel that love for Daddy was the only crime that was committed by those involved and closest to him.

What I do believe happened was that as a county commissioner of Jefferson County, Daddy had access to power, money, and influence. He worked to bring about change in the county and in our town. With one phone call, he could see that things were changed or rectified for its citizens for the better. For example, I know of one family who had a serious plumbing issue and had to have their whole front yard dug up. Daddy called and asked some of his friends to go help them. It would have cost the family thousands of dollars they didn't have, but he got it done for them at a greatly reduced cost. He helped a lot of people that way.

I heard him telling someone that he had power over millions of dollars and could dictate how it was spent. That's amazing for a Black man who came from where he did to have that kind of influence and power. People should also understand Daddy was a man whose daughter was tragically killed in the bombing. There wasn't anyone in this town who didn't feel for him because of that, or who didn't respect him for the way he handled it. He didn't incite people to riot during that time, but in fact pleaded with people to stay calm and not behave badly just because others had. That gained him respect in the white community as well as the Black community, because he handled it all well.

That being said, fast-forward to when Spike Lee directed and released the documentary *4 Little Girls*. Daddy had spent decades working in the legislature and the county, and had made many white friends, attended Rotary Club, was a photographer, and had taken pictures in many people's homes. When the documentary came out, people reflected, perhaps for the first time, on the price Daddy had paid. Some people thought, "We know Chris McNair likes us and he's nice. How in the world could he be as nice as he was to us after that tragedy?" I am not making this up, because I had many white people say it to me. They were amazed by his grace and kindness.

Daddy's business clients and friends were invited to the premiere of the film when it was held here in Birmingham, along with hundreds of other people. They watched the story of their friend's child who was murdered. It caused people to wonder what they would have done if it had happened to them, and some concluded they could not have done what Daddy did.

Those were some of the same people who did business with him in the county. After seeing that documentary, they were asking, "What can we do for Chris? He has always been there for us." He was old and getting ready to retire, so they wanted to do whatever they could to help him out. They knew he wanted to add an art gallery to his business, but he couldn't get a loan because his credit was over-extended. As I said before, he wasn't the best businessman. So his friends got together and decided they were going to do something for Chris—they were going to help him build the gallery.

There was no quid pro quo. These people had been getting business done within the county for decades. They are some of the same people who were like family and who came to have Thanksgiving and Easter dinners with us, and who spent time with us in our home and we in theirs. We'd go to weddings and funerals for each other's family members together. The problem was they happened to be people who still did business with the county, and that was not allowed, because Daddy was a public official. They helped him get the financing for the gallery and to get it built. Daddy didn't give them any business because they were already doing business for the county. What many people don't know is that Daddy had a tendency to be very frugal, some say cheap. He was really cautious with money. There was even a comment in the newspaper once about how frugal Daddy was with the county's money and how he would not spend any more on things than was absolutely necessary. He was also like that at home. He rarely bought anything that we didn't absolutely need. I remember in the 1970s, they came out with generic food products that were versions of the grocery store brand items that you could buy much cheaper. They were even packaged inexpensively in very nondescript white boxes with black writing that just said "butter," "cheese," "corn flakes," and "detergent," just to name a few. We were very rarely allowed to splurge on anything because we just didn't have the money.

I suppose someone looked at the gallery on a main thoroughfare and wondered who the contractor and the construction company were. People started asking questions, reaching their own conclusions, and eventually someone must have said something didn't add up. Possibly some of the people who wanted county business but didn't get it were upset, so they told others, and that's how the federal investigators got involved. That's how Daddy got into trouble.

Did he take the help from people he wasn't supposed to? Yes. Was there a quid pro quo? No. Was it wrong? Yes, because that's what the law says. Was there malice? NO! Neither was there greed or graft. Even so, Daddy was sentenced to five years in federal prison. He was in his mid eighties when he went away and had suffered a stroke. He was also ordered to pay $800,000 in restitution, which he is still paying off. This really broke him as a man. He was never the same afterward.

It is because of you that Daddy got out of prison a little early. The fiftieth anniversary of the church bombing was coming up in 2013, when Daddy was still in prison. I suspected that no one would want it known that the father of one of the little girls, who had served his community with distinction, was in prison, and I was correct. Two weeks before the anniversary, Daddy was released, thanks to an edict for older prisoners from President Obama.

The fiftieth anniversary of your death was a huge event for the city. Lots of local and national press and many activities surrounded that date. I can't tell you how many news outlets reached out to me for interviews. It reminded people of the tragedy that happened fifty years earlier. Other people today did not even know about it. By this time Daddy and Mamma were unable to be interviewed as they were both suffering from different forms of dementia. I was more comfortable talking to the press than Kim, so she and I decided that I would be the primary spokesperson for our family.

One big project that took place was building statues to honor you and the other girls. Two local people headed that project up: a local lawyer named Chervis

These are the beautiful statues erected in honor of you, Carole, Addie Mae, and Cynthia in September 2013. They sit in Kelly Ingram Park, diagonally across the street from the 16th Street Baptist Church where your life was taken. Photo by Lisa McNair.

Isom and Carolyn McKinstry. You probably remember her as Carolyn Maull. She attended 16th Street Church and was friends with Addie Mae, Cynthia, and Carole. They did a wonderful job of involving the families in choosing the artist and the design for the statues. You are in a prominent place on this wonderful piece of art. I believe everyone was pleased at how it turned out. The statues sit right in front of Kelly Ingram Park, facing the church. When I pass by them, I like to watch other people as they are viewing the statues. It is interesting to watch everyone's reactions. Sometimes I will walk up to them, introduce myself, and tell them a little bit about you. Other times I just stand around and listen to what they say to one another.

Another fantastic thing that took place for the fiftieth anniversary is that you and the other girls were posthumously given the Congressional Gold Medal. It is the highest honor that a person or institution can receive from Congress. Two congresspeople from Alabama wrote the bill for you to receive this honor: Terri Sewell, who is our only Black and only Democratic congressperson, and Spencer Bacchus, who is white and a Republican. I am proud of the fact that they were able to come together and do that. Once the bill was written, both houses of Congress approved it. The next step was for it to be signed by the president. Our president at the time was Barack Obama, our first African American president. Mamma and I got to fly to Washington, DC, to see him sign the bill. It was an

The front and back of the Congressional Gold Medal. The families were allowed to choose the design on the coin from a variety of artist drawings from the US Mint. Photo by Lisa McNair.

AMAZING experience. I could hardly believe it. In fact, when the representative from Terri Sewell's office called me, I didn't believe it was really going to happen. She had to scream at me for it to finally sink in. I could not have been more excited.

It was May 2013 when Mamma and I flew up to Washington, DC. Along with several other people—Doug Jones, who prosecuted the last two killers, Carole's sister Dianne Robertson Braddock, and Congresswoman Sewell—we went to the Oval Office and met President Obama. He was very kind and gracious, really down-to-earth. He welcomed us all in his office and asked us to stand behind his desk in the Oval. Then he walked in front of the desk and thanked us all for being there and for the supreme sacrifice that the families unwillingly made in the fight for freedom. He also expressed his gratitude and stated that without Civil Rights incidents like the bombing he would not be where he is today. It was very moving. He then came back around the desk, pulled Mamma, who was in a

In the Oval Office in 2013 as President Obama signs the bill for the Congressional Gold Medal. From left to right: Surgeon General Regina Benjamin, Birmingham Mayor William Bell, Sharon Holder, US Attorney General Eric Holder, Congresswoman Terri Sewell, President Barack Obama, Maxine McNair (Mamma), me, Dianne Robertson Braddock, Pastor Arthur Price (current pastor of 16th Street Baptist Church), and attorney Doug Jones, who prosecuted the surviving killers. The White House Office of Photography.

wheelchair, close to him and started the signing ceremony. The press was allowed to come in. It was amazing, dozens of reporters piled in and began taking pictures in rapid succession. It was so crazy. Then the president spoke again about the significance of the moment and signed the bill. It was a surreal moment in time that I will never forget.

Of course, Mamma really missed Daddy while he was away. It was bad for all of us, and terribly embarrassing. We made three trips up to see him. It was a crazy experience, traveling all that way with Mamma, who at that time was using a walker and sometimes a wheelchair. She had lost most of her sight and had Alzheimer's disease. As I said, after Daddy got out, he was still paying off his fines. He also lost his right to vote until they were paid off. He never voted again. That only added to the depression he was in. But it was great to have him back home. We tried to make him as happy as we could. His health was failing and he was not doing well as I wrote this.

Much love,
Lisa

Dogs Have Always Been My Closest Friends

Dear Denise,

I know I am repeating myself, but bear with me. In our neighborhood growing up, there were quite a few boys but not many little girls with whom I could play. Therefore, I spent a lot of time alone as a child. It wasn't bad, really. Early in my life, your friends and our neighbors, Cynthia and Yolanda Northrup, Rhonda and Barbara Nunn, Vicki and Rochelle Smith, and Ethel Ross and Debra Bird would come by the house and play with me. They missed you and it helped them to come around to see Mamma and me. They were so much fun, but eventually they all were involved in high school and then off to college. Our younger sister, Kimberly, was born four years after me, so it was some time before she was old enough to play with.

I have mentioned that there were two little girls in the neighborhood with whom I could play. One was Lynn Williams and the other was Robin Reynolds—we called her Lane. Lane lived up the street near the railroad tracks. It was awhile before Mamma would let me walk that far. Lane's house was fun to go to because she had lots of brothers and sisters.

Her mom, Miss Sudie Bee, was always nice to me and would treat me like one of her own. Lane was painfully shy, but we played well together. Every time she was over to my house to play, eventually she would start to cry and run home. Mamma would ask me if I had said something to hurt her feelings, and I would always respond, "No ma'am!" I always wondered why she did that. Recently, I asked her and, funnily enough, she didn't remember doing that. She said she was probably sad because she knew she would have to leave and go home soon anyway.

Being an only child for so long, I often played by myself. I thought of you and wondered what it would have been like to have you around. When I look back, however, my best friends were not the children in the neighborhood but rather our dogs! Daddy loves dogs and he passed that love on to me. You left two sweet dogs behind, Big Whitey and Little Whitey. After they died, we got Brownie, who was a poodle. He was too cute, but kept running away. We didn't have a very secure fence for our backyard.

You in our front yard with your dog Big Whitey. Photo by Chris McNair.

I loved going out in the yard to play with the dogs, and I could play with them for hours, or just sit and talk with them. They seemed to know what I was thinking and feeling, and they knew how to make me feel better if I was having a bad day. In the ensuing years, they brought me comfort because they accepted me when other adults and kids didn't, and they liked me no matter what. They never said, "You are not Black enough," or "You act like a white girl." My dogs were my very best friends. They were always happy to see me.

Years later when I was working in the family business, I was asked by a lady who did some work for us if I would like to be on the board of a nonprofit organization for which she volunteered called Hand in Paw. When she told me Hand in Paw trained volunteers and their animals to go out to hospitals, nursing homes, and schools to provide animal-assisted therapy, I was super-excited. My dogs had been giving me animal-assisted therapy for years, and I never knew what they did for me had a name.

She said they were looking for more diversity on their board, which, loosely translated, meant they needed some Black folks. That was fine with me, because this was an organization that I could support. And if I had to be the token Black person, I was willing to do so. As I've already told you, years later, when the studio was going out of business, I applied for a job at Hand in Paw and they hired me. I worked there for fifteen years. It was one of the biggest blessings of my life to work for an organization with such a great mission. I met so many wonderful people among the volunteers who carry out Hand in Paw's mission; they were heaven-sent.

I guess that proves that God is preparing us for our purpose even when we are not aware that He is. Those lonely years when I learned to play with our dogs were prepping me for my work at Hand in Paw. We now have a dog named Banjo, and I would take him to work with me. That was another blessing of working there: you could bring your dog to work. He loves to ride in the car with me and is good company when I get lonely, which isn't often. He loves to come to my apartment. Banjo was a stray that just showed up in our yard. He was very sick when we took him in and had to live in the house because our other dogs, Zeus and Apollo, didn't like him. They live in the back yard; Banjo is our first housedog and is so spoiled.

I had hoped Banjo could be a therapy animal with Hand in Paw, but he does show some aggression every now and then toward other dogs (though he loves people). To qualify as a therapy pet, a dog must have a special set of characteristics. Sadly, Banjo doesn't make the grade. Zeus and Apollo will also never be confused with therapy animals; they don't like animals *or* people. They are good guard dogs, though, and they along with Banjo are great therapy for me.

I like to think that all our dogs that have passed on are in heaven with you and that you watch over them. Give each one of them a hug for me—Big Whitey, Little Whitey, Brownie, Scotty, Tracey, Cleo, Forniss, Rusty, Jewel (my precious Jewel), Princess, Mufasa, Diva, Venus, and Serena. I'll see you all one day.

Love,
Lisa

Crazy Stuff People Say

Dear Denise,

I've told you about my white friends and how for years I related better to white people than Black. That doesn't mean that I haven't had my share of troubles with white folks. Of course, my troubles compared to your troubles are no troubles at all, but they still serve to remind me that at the end of the day, some people do see color and they still don't know how to act.

For example, one of my coworkers' husbands would come in the office from time to time to help us with things. We locked something up in a cabinet one day and couldn't find the key to get in. So he asked his wife to ask me if I could pick the lock. I guess he thought he was being funny, but the implication was clear: he thought Black people have a propensity for breaking into places, so let's ask Lisa because that must be a skill she has. I didn't think it was funny and no, I don't know how to pick a lock.

Then I worked with another white woman who was the kind of white woman who would find a Black person she loved and assign herself to look after me like I was a little puppy. She proceeded to say and do all kinds of inappropriate things, but she had no clue they were offensive. She thought I thought like she did, so she felt free to say what was on her mind, without any regard for my feelings.

As the executive assistant my director would ask me to do various tasks for her. I thought that was part of my job; plus we were friends and I didn't mind helping her out. Often it got me out of the office. But this woman who "adopted" me did not like her asking me to run her errands. She said that my boss was treating me like I was her "little slave." And I was just thinking, "Really? Even if you thought that, did you have to say it out loud where other people could hear it? Did she have to use that word?" When something like that is said to me, I don't know what to do or say. Do I confront it? Say something? Smile and laugh it off? I don't mind when white people ask me about an issue in the Black community that they don't understand. I *want* them to ask me. I'd rather them hear it from me than go out and make some silly faux pas. But to say something like that is just inappropriate.

A few years ago, I decided there was some stuff about white people that I really wanted to know, so I just started asking them. I worked in an office of seven people and everyone else is white. All my life I heard white people talk about going to the lake, so I asked, "Where is the lake? Y'all are always going to the lake. What's the big deal about going to the lake?" I asked why they always say they are going to "the lake" as if it is only one lake, and not a bunch of different ones.

I asked a former boss why a lot of little white children, especially babies, didn't seem to ever wear shoes. I assumed it must be a white thing, because we put shoes on our children. My boss at the time said they were taught that kids who didn't wear shoes were healthier, because their feet were exposed. She said she was told that it would boost their immune systems. I thought that was interesting—a little odd, but interesting. Diversity should be funny at some point and not a controversial or painful thing. Heck, our people didn't wear shoes for generations because we didn't have any.

There are times when I do get upset, but not often. Recently I had dinner with some of my Black friends. They are good people who are funny, and they make me laugh. They are unique friends. They have high profile jobs and get to do a lot of varied things and go to different places I don't get to go, so that makes them interesting. Most of them have master's degrees or even PhDs. It is fascinating talking with them.

In talking about our weekend plans at one gathering, I mentioned that I was going to a bar mitzvah. One of my friends said, "Are you Black for real?" I laughed because it was funny to me too. My Black friends and family all my life have asked me that question in one way or another.

That night after I left them and went home, however, I began to get that old feeling I had from my youth and became angry over what she had said. Why couldn't I go to a bar mitzvah? Did only white or Jewish folks get to attend those events? Why didn't they find that to be interesting and say something like "Really? I have never been to one. I wonder what it will be like?"

Then I relived all the times growing up I was called "white girl" or accused of "acting white." Even at my age today, that still gets on my nerves when I hear it. Couldn't Black folks simply say, "That is a very different cultural experience than I have had. How interesting for you to get an opportunity to go do that," or "I'd like to go with you. I have never been to one of those events."

The night conjured up all those old feelings of not fitting in with my African

American culture for so many years and being able to relate more to white culture than Black culture.

I have told you that when I was growing up, we had a lot of white friends and acquaintances in and out of our house. At that time in the South, the races spending time together socially was just not the norm. Daddy being a member of a Lutheran church wasn't a very "Black" thing to do in the South. If you were Black, you were usually Baptist, Pentecostal, CME (Christian Methodist Episcopal), or AME (African Methodist Episcopal).

People make comments like, "you don't know enough Black stuff." Those people are correct—there are some things I don't know, but I am constantly trying to learn more about all things. While we are on that subject, let me tell you a funny story. A few years ago, our brother-in-law, Jimmie (you would like him; he has an unusual sense of humor), and I were talking, and he was saying something about a Black comedian named Katt Williams.

I should have asked Jimmie to refresh my memory instead of saying, "tell me about her again." To this day, my brother-in-law will not let me live that down because I didn't know who *he*, not she, was. He said, "you are so *not* Black. You don't know Katt Williams is a he and a famous comedian." I was embarrassed at first but later realized how funny it was. I had heard of him, but only once and it had slipped my mind. We often laugh about that now.

I don't get angry about these things anymore. I am more comfortable with who I am now, how I was raised, and my unique life experience than I ever have been before. I had a few life epiphanies, moments of insight that helped put my struggles and my place in proper perspective. Let me share a few of those with you soon. Right now, I must go help Kim with Mamma and Daddy, and I am running late.

Love you,
Lisa

Glory

Dear Denise,

When I was in the first grade, we started each day by reciting the pledge of allegiance to the American flag and then the Lord's Prayer. Growing up, we also had to memorize the national anthem, as I'm sure you did. In school, we learned about American history, but most of what I learned was about Caucasian people, with very little emphasis on what contributions Black people had brought to this country.

It is etched in my memory that George Washington was our first president who chopped down a cherry tree and confessed his guilt when confronted. I learned that Benjamin Franklin discovered electricity, Abraham Lincoln freed the slaves, Alexander Graham Bell invented the telephone, Thomas Edison developed the light bulb, and JFK was one of the greatest presidents we ever had. We also learned that Christopher Columbus discovered America and was from Spain, and we all learned to sing, "Columbus sailed the ocean blue in 1400 and '92."

All these historical figures were white people. I didn't resent them for doing what they did, but it always made me think: Where were my people? What were we doing while they created our country and culture? Did we contribute in any way? Was our only claim to fame being slaves? In addition to Harriet Tubman creating the Underground Railroad and Martin Luther King Jr. helping us to gain Civil Rights, where were we? What did we do? Were we kept out of the entire process?

I grew up knowing that my life had value because Mamma and my family instilled that in me. I knew on paper that I was an American, but I never really felt that I was a truly an American. My white contemporaries got excited about the Fourth of July, Memorial Day, and Veterans Day. They talked openly about grandfathers and fathers who served in World War I and World War II. I never felt that I could participate in the celebrations. Even though Daddy also served in one of those wars, I didn't even realize that until later in life. I don't believe he saw combat. He never talked about his experience other than to explain that it took time out from college so he graduated a few years later than planned. I never thought about celebrating his making it back home and the fact that if he had not come back, I would not be here. He probably didn't celebtate his return from the war because our country didn't celebrate our returning warriors of color when they came home. They fought for freedom but had very little when they returned home. I recently saw a very moving documentary titled *The Blinding of Isaac Woodard* that talked about how white men were intimidated by the return of Black soldiers because they had tasted freedom; white people didn't want them to come back and demand rights they were not given in the states. The documentary told the story of a soldier who was on a bus returning home from the war who was beaten; he had his eye gouged out because his attackers didn't like the fact that he was fraternizing with the white soldiers on the bus. It was horrible. He did nothing wrong and was in his uniform when he was beaten. It was a terrible thing to happen in this country that claims to be the land of the free and the home of the brave.

For me, I saw our experience here in America as quite sad and even tragic. My African ancestors were brought here against their will from their home and everything they knew, and were forced to be slaves—the lowest form of human existence in this country. They were taught to forget their heritage and all they knew. History books never showed that we had a part in helping ourselves to be free. Even after we were free, we were enslaved in another way for the next 100 years through segregation and Jim Crow laws.

Then I saw a movie called *Glory*. It was the true story of the Fifty-Fourth Massachusetts Infantry Regiment, made up entirely of Black Union soldiers who fought in the Civil War. I loved that movie because I got to see Black people fighting for freedom in the War between the States. I did not realize any of our people had fought because we were not taught that in school. When I left that movie, I was filled with the thought that we, Black folks, really do matter. We helped make this country, and it is our country, just like it is for white folks. We helped build the infrastructure of this nation. It was our blood, sweat, and tears that made much of it happen. I am not trying to cut white people out, because they worked too. Their story was told on a regular basis, however, while our story was told rarely, if at all.

Today we celebrate Black History Month in February. It's a time when television, radio, schools, churches, and communities tell stories of our heritage and some of our people who helped make this nation great—people like James Baldwin, W. E. B. Du Bois, Sojourner Truth, A. Philip Randolph, Thurgood Marshall, and so many others who are not well known because they were seldom if ever mentioned in school books. Black History Month was recognized in some places when you were alive, but certainly not in Alabama. Today, it's a big deal here and everywhere.

It's funny that it took a movie to wake me up to the significance of my own people, but however it happened, I'm glad it did. You, my sister, are part of that Black history too.

Love you,
Lisa

9/11

Dear Denise,

I know you were aware that growing up Black in America was tough, and I have to tell you—it still has its challenges. When I grew up, there were almost no images of Black folks on television, newspapers and magazines. When someone used the phrase "All-American," they often meant baseball, apple pie, and a white child. Never any reference to people of color. I already told you about the impact the movie *Glory* had on me, because I got to see that Black people fought for freedom in the War between the States just like white folks did. For me, that meant this is really our country too. It was the first time I felt ownership of the country, and that I belonged just like any other American.

Denise, on September 11, 2001, some crazy foreign terrorists hijacked some airplanes and flew them into the World Trade Center buildings in New York and the Pentagon, near Washington, DC. Another plane crashed in Pennsylvania; we suspect it was headed for either the White House or the US Capitol. Nearly 3,000 people perished. The whole country felt terrorized that day. We now refer to that day as 9/11 and, as bad as it was, it really drove home the fact that we are *all* Americans. Anyone who is coming to get us is coming to get us all. They aren't coming to get just white people, they were coming to get ALL Americans: Black, white, and any other race that is considered an American citizen—they didn't discriminate. When I went to the 9/11 Memorial in New York City, I saw that all races of people were memorialized there: Black, white, Asian, Hispanic, Middle Eastern . . . everyone.

What happened on 9/11, like what happened to you, was pure evil. Everyone who was old enough to remember that day has a story of what they were doing when the planes hit. I was working for our family business that day and was moving slowly that morning. I had the TV on, and a report said that two planes had hit the twin towers. I said, "Oh, my God. This is an attack against our country. That was not an accident!" I finished getting dressed and went to work.

I needed to get gas before I went to the office. By the time I got to the gas station, the Pentagon had been hit by a plane too. We were under attack as Americans.

We were officially under attack, there was no doubt about it. While at the gas station, there was a white guy who was pumping gas next to me (yes, in most states in America we pump our own gas today; no one does it for us), and I thought, "today it doesn't matter who we are. We are under attack because we are Americans." The race thing seemed so unimportant at that moment because some individuals from another country hated us enough to want to take us out, and they were coming for all of *us*.

When you were killed, people didn't think like that. They thought more in terms of "Black and white." On 9/11, however, we thought as Americans, and maybe it shows how far we have come. I hope so. We always need to remember that we are one country, together.

Love ya,
Lisa

Racial Issues

Dear Denise,

I can't imagine how it was when you were a girl, but today at least some people talk about racial issues openly and with some degree of honesty. For as long as I can remember, I have been fascinated by race and racial issues, but we didn't talk much about any of that when I was a girl—mostly because it was so prominent in our family after your death.

We never even talked about obvious things. For example, we knew that white slave masters raped or had relations with their slave women. It always intrigued me that people didn't think or talk about that. How else do they think we all came in so many different shades and colors with so many different hair textures?

There was a senator from South Carolina named Strom Thurmond. He was elected to the Senate when you were a toddler and stayed until his death in 2003! He was a staunch segregationist, but after his death it was revealed that he had fathered a child with a Black teenager who worked for his parents. Some people were shocked! We also learned that President Thomas Jefferson had children with his slave Sally Hemings. None of that surprised me, even when other people acted surprised and agitated about it. It made all the news broadcasts and newspapers. That was something we never used to talk about, but it's been going on for a long time. It is very sad that these women had no control over what happened to their bodies. They were just objects to be used and abused. It is devastating to think about.

When you think of it, some of our own relatives tended to be a little lighter. I was told you had gray eyes. Mamma's aunt on her dad's side of her family had red hair. How did she get that red hair? We talk more openly about it now, but there are plenty of racial matters that we still don't talk about. We talk about them among ourselves in the Black community, but it didn't seem to be widely known among the white community. Maybe they aren't ready to acknowledge that we are more related to one another than just as human beings!

I don't have the anger, fear, or resentment toward white people that the generation before me and many since have had. I don't have the personal experiences to support that kind of anger, although I have every right to be angry over what happened to you. That was something I struggled with early in life, as I have shared with you earlier. When I would bring my white friends around some of my Black friends, those Black friends were cordial but they couldn't understand why those people were my friends. They would think or act like, "Why don't you dislike them like we do?" I couldn't do that because I had too many white friends who I know were not racist. I came to see them as just people like us. I still can't go there; it's not even an option. Just as I don't want them to hate us, I can't hate them. Are there still racist white folks around? Yes, and there always will be, but we must love them as Christ loved us and try to change their thinking. Don't think that I don't get angry or dislike their behavior, but treating them like they would treat me will not help foster unity in this country. I choose to abide by Dr. King's Fifth Principle of Nonviolence, which says, "Nonviolence chooses love instead of hate." I just cannot see living any other way.

Getting back to our relatives, our cousin Marty, one of seven children, married a white girl. Out of his six siblings, only one of them married a Black person. One is not married at all, but he mostly dates white women. The oldest brother lived with an Asian woman for fifteen years. The oldest sister married a man of Japanese and white ancestry; he was Jewish, although he converted to Christianity. The baby boy plays in a well-known rock band and is married to a Norwegian woman. As you can see, as a family we are all over the place racially. There are more family members who have married interracially. I have always felt if we could love each other, we could not hate each other.

I wish you were here so we could talk about this. I'm sure it would blow your mind how openly we talk about things compared to when you were living. Yet in my opinion, we still are not as open about racial issues as we need to be. We need to broaden those conversations.

Miss you,
Lisa

Our Black Heritage

Dear Denise,

We have talked a lot about how I was raised as an African American woman in this white culture. I am thinking about putting these letters in book form so that anyone who has Black kids going to a mostly white school can read it. Then maybe they will understand the reason why their Black children know only a little about Black heritage, which isn't being taught in their schools. Then they will understand why their children are so open to and saturated with white cultural norms. Their parents can also learn how to help them to navigate in this new world. It might help those kids feel less alone, as well.

The subtle prejudice against things Black is easy to assimilate because it's all around us. For me, it started in second grade when Harriett asked, "Who's lighter?" In her mind, and in the minds of many of African Americans, being dark skinned was not good. The general perception is that the lighter you were, the better you were. This is because white was the best in the minds of many in our country, so a lighter Black person would be closer to looking like a white person, which was the ultimate goal of perfection.

Another subtle form of African American self-denigration was to put ourselves down in the same ways that we have heard the white race do. For example, I sometimes heard family members say, "A lie ain't nothing for a nigger to tell." They were referring to other Black folks when they would say that. We have used that horrible word, "nigger," against our own people, and that always makes me sad. Or someone would do something wrong and people would say, "Black people don't act right anyway." We often indicted ourselves because, even though we were Black, we were downing other Black people and disrespecting our own Black culture. This, sometimes unbeknownst to us, has created a feeling of self-loathing that most of us don't even realize.

Our parents worked hard to give us a better life, as did other Black parents from our parents' generation. They worked hard to provide a better life than the one they had, which included homes in white suburbs that had predominately white schools. They wanted a better education for their children—and often that education was to be found in the white schools, since many of the schools in the Black areas of town were often denied the resources that the white schools were given. Dr. King's dream was to see integration as a common occurrence, but that integration caused an erosion of Black identity and an ignorance of Black history and culture for those kids like myself who spent a great deal of time in a mostly white world.

That's why I work as hard as I do on behalf of an organization by the name of Sojourn into the Past. Sojourn takes high schoolers through the American South and teaches students in a mobile classroom about the Civil Rights Movement and our Black history that often isn't taught sufficiently in schools and is almost completely absent in the schoolbooks. When that isn't taught, the Black kids aren't learning who they are and where they came from. They aren't learning the strong heritage of our people who made a life for themselves in this country, despite tremendous odds against them. Neither do the white kids learn about our strong heritage and see a positive side of our people. They may be learning Christian values and all the "correct" things, but they are also learning that all things white people do are right and all things Black people do are wrong. They need to learn the whole story and not just the parts that are easy to hear.

While I was growing up, I had the privilege of seeing Black people all around me who were heroes in everyday life: people like Daddy who built a successful life and career in a segregated world, along with other family members who were successful businessmen and women or who received high levels of education and had successful careers as professionals. Many white kids do not get to see Black people positioned as heroes in the same way I always did.

White students need to learn the stories of hard-working Black people in their history lessons. After all, Black history is our shared American History. We cannot teach one without teaching the other. White kids as well as Black kids and students of all races need to know that African Americans did great things to make our country the wonderful place it is now. We all did it together; Black, white, Hispanic, Asian, and Native American. The full American history must be taught in schools, not just part of it.

I also am on the board of an organization called the Morgan Project that is working toward this goal. We are working to update the curriculum that is taught in all Alabama schools to include our rich Civil Rights history along with the current history that is being taught. It is our hope that the whole story of Alabama's history can be taught in order that all students can learn our full and right history. The Morgan Project was named after Charles Morgan, a white man who spoke up at the Birmingham Young Men's Business Club meeting the day after you were killed. He said that members of the city's white upper class were just as much responsible for your death as avowed racists and Klansmen because they allowed the powers that be to continue the segregated laws and practices in Birmingham and remained silent. Sadly, following his speech, he and his family were run out of town because he was brave and spoke the truth. He wrote an amazing book called *A Time to Speak*, and we have based our curriculum on it. He was so brave to no longer be a silent witness but to speak up about a wrong he saw in our city.

On a side note, I appreciate interracial or white couples who adopt African American children, but that relationship makes me nervous because of one issue: Those parents have a responsibility to make sure that both halves of their children's lives are being taught. Biracial children need to see their Black family members as often as their white family members, especially if their social interaction in everyday life is with more white people than Black. That's why I am committed to the lessons taught by Sojourn into the Past. Here is a description of their mission statement from their website:

> Sojourn to the Past is an award-winning, nationally recognized Civil Rights Movement educational program that is aligned with state and national curriculum standards. The program provides participants with an opportunity to earn college credit and is made available to underserved students. The journey is a life-changing experience for our participants, and we have led thousands of students through the hallowed sites of the Freedom Struggle.

I enjoy having the freedom to build relationships with whomever I feel comfortable as an African American woman—that was part of Dr. King's dream. My relationships don't have to be either white or Black, and can (and should) be both. As a Black woman, I should make sure that they are both, or I can pick up on the subtle cultural nuance that says, "white is better" or "Black only." White is not better; it's just different. Black is not better, it's just different. But together, we are *great*!

As much as I enjoyed my life and as much as I wouldn't take anything from that Advent experience, I thank God I came from a household where I could not turn my back on my Blackness, even when it crossed my mind. Even though there was a lot of white going on, I couldn't turn my back completely on who we are because of you and the price that our family paid to be Black and live in Alabama. I didn't really start to appreciate my own heritage until years later, in my late thirties.

Does any of this make sense? It does to me, but it took me a long time to figure it out. I only wish you had been here to talk these things over, face to face.

I miss you, girl,
Lisa

We Aren't So Different

Dear Denise,

I've already mentioned that a common misconception in some parts of Black society is that all things white are automatically better: that they are nicer people, smarter, and work harder. There is even a perception among us that life doesn't seem to be as hard for them. We assume that, I suppose, from watching so much television that portrays many white people as successful—although that has changed recently. Also, this is perpetuated by the past history of how well they lived compared to our people. Many of our people worked in nice white homes and because they lived so well, we believed that everything white was better, nicer, the right things to have, be, and do.

I was liberated when I realized this was not true. In more ways than not, we are all alike, all just human beings. I came to this realization by observing many aspects of life that were common to us all. I watched white folks in the workplace. We as a people try even harder to do our best around white folks so they would see our worth and value. I used to think they didn't make mistakes, got up earlier for work, and always did things right. I was so glad to know they made mistakes too, and some of them are even lazy and don't want to work!

I employed an accountant who did the books for our business. He was a very nice white guy, and was also an excellent accountant. Yet that man could never be on time for an appointment. I mean he was *always* late. My sister and I would always laugh and say that he was on "CP" time, which is "colored-people" time.

Then I learned the term "poor white trash" later in life. It helped me realize that even within the white community there were factions, divisions, and prejudices, just like we had established with the light skinned, dark skinned issue. They may have felt superior to African Americans, but they had their own issues of separation among themselves.

What we all have in common, white and Black, is our personal pain. I have gone to many white people's funerals over the years and learned that sorrow has no color. I have gone to the family hours when families meet with friends and the friends can view the body of the deceased. The sorrow was so thick, it could be cut with a knife, because everyone was painfully aware that their friend or loved one would never walk with them on Earth again. Loss is loss. It has no color or race.

Some of them have been taken away too soon. Some have gone home after a long and painful illness. In either case, the sorrow is real and true and knows no color. I have seen my white friends with red faces and wet, swollen eyes, asking the same things that my folks ask when we lose a loved one. They are searching for the answer to the questions "Why?" and "What are we going to do now?" There is no Black or white, just grief, sorrow, and a desperate need for healing and consolation.

I don't take any pleasure in their sorrow, but I do find a peace in knowing that we all feel the same thing and that we are not different. All hearts grieve and experience sorrow and disappointment. It is the same when we lose a job, have an accident, or can't pay bills. All sorts of situations bring pain and disappointment that are common to humans, no matter our race or color. For that reason alone, we should draw close and be more kind to one another.

I wonder what your experience was with white folks when you were growing up? I would love to talk with you about that. Guess I will add that to the list of questions to ask you when I get to heaven.

Love you,
Lisa

Daddy Is with You Now

Dear Denise,

On a warm, sunny day in May 2019, Daddy left this earthly world to join you and our Father in Heaven. I knew one day he would have to leave us, but it is still hard to believe he is gone. I was there with him, holding his hand to help him know everything was going to be all right. I thanked him for a lifetime of being there for me; for teaching so many wonderful lessons about life and how to be a strong Black woman. He was tough even to the end. I play that afternoon over and over again in my mind. I wish I could have done more for him, but I know that it was his time.

His last few years were sad ones. He had been through a great deal, but sadly in those latter years he didn't bounce back. He was so sad and depressed most of the time. Often being with him was heartbreaking even before his diagnosis of terminal cancer. By the time they diagnosed him, they told us he had only two weeks to live, or a short month at most. The news was overwhelming to hear, almost too much to take in at one time. It caused us to work quickly to see if we could do whatever he needed to make him happy and to be comfortable. The doctor told us not to tell him, so we didn't. It seemed wrong; I think I would want to know so that I could plan to do anything I had not done or share anything I had not said. But we followed the doctor's advice. We quickly went into action and contacted as many people as we could and asked them to come see him. It was the best medicine of all. People came from far and near. People we had not seen in years came to visit him. People who had been in that terrible trouble with him from the county came by every day. Daddy loved being around people and these visits gave him life. It was wonderful. Although we were losing him, God gave him back to us for a few short weeks. Before the diagnosis he was so depressed. There didn't seem to be anything we could do to lift him up. But now, he was not depressed anymore. He was happy. He talked more and seemed to be more alert. It was like having the old Daddy back. It made Kim and me feel so good to see him like that. It gave us hope that he might live longer than the doctor said. We had missed the way Daddy used to be. His words were the best part of him. He always had something to say that was wise and made you think. In fact, one of his favorite sayings

Mamma and Daddy at his ninetieth birthday party. Photo by Audra Gray.

was, "THINK!! Always be thinking." But as the days went on the pain began to take hold of his body. That made me so sad. He fought it like a champ. He didn't want to take the pain medicine but sometimes it was too much. He was a tough old bird, even until the end.

I have a video Kim shot of him the morning of the day he died. His voice was still strong. I played it over and over again after he died. I just wanted to hear his voice again. As you know he had the most amazing voice; it was very deep, strong, and powerful, even at the end. We also took pictures with almost everyone who came to see him. They warm our heart when we look at them.

I have never seen anyone die before. Part of me did not want to see him take his last breath; it's something you can never forget once you see it. But I thought if it were me, I would want someone to be with me as I left this earth; someone who loved and cared for me so that I would feel safe and not be scared. When he let out that last breath, I knew he was gone. There was an odd peace about it. He had run his race, finished his course and now his time was done. Kim came in and spent some time with him. The hospice people took over; they cleaned him up, put on a new T-shirt, and sat him up in the bed. We brought Mamma in and told her that Daddy had passed. We were not sure how she would take this now that she was far into her Alzheimer's disease and was legally blind. She said "WHAT??!!! Chris is dead??!!!" We sat her by him and she rubbed his head and said, "awe, Chris, you weren't supposed to leave me." That was it; I had to leave the room. I left Kim and the home health care workers in the room with her. I really didn't have much time to cry. I had to jump into action. I called our Uncle Harold, Daddy's brother who lived in Birmingham, and told him. He was so strong but very sad. That was truly a call I didn't want to make. I asked him to please share the news with the family.

There were a number of key people that I had to notify, so I began making calls and texting. My dear friend Anil was with me. He met me at the house and was there to support me when Daddy died. Once I got the call from Kim that this might be the end, I let Anil know that Daddy might be dying. He dropped everything to be there. He grew to love Daddy while he worked as one of the lawyers on his trial. Daddy meant the world to him. We have some of the same friends, like Doug Jones and Reena Evers-Everette, so he began helping me call them. I was concerned that the news would get wind of it before I had a chance to get a press release out. You see, Denise, Daddy dying was front-page news. So I called a friend and asked her to write a press release for me. The crazy thing about that is before I could hang up with her, someone had already posted condolences on my Facebook page. Daddy died at about 3:30 p.m. I didn't make the 5:00 o'clock news, but it was already going to be the lead story on the 6:00 o'clock news, as they had a blurb about it during the commercial break in the 5:30 broadcast. I got our press release out just in time to be read on the 6:00 news on all our local affiliates. I didn't even think about sending it out to my national news friends, but it got out somehow. The next few hours were wild. We were busy calling family and close friends. I received so many texts and voice mail messages that it took two days to respond to most of them. The caregiver, for some odd reason, had called people and was taking them into the bedroom to see Daddy. To this day, I don't know who those folks were. I was so shocked that I didn't tell her to stop. Kim was in the room with him so I knew if it had been a problem, she would have said something. A few close friends and family members came by. Two of my closest friends, Wendy and Octavia, came by and stayed with me most of the evening to support me. Several of Kim's close friends came by as well.

They didn't take Daddy's body away for several hours. The hospice folks told us to take as long as we needed. Mamma stayed with him for about an hour. We waited for our Uncle Harold and Aunt Vivian to come. I knew they would want to see him. Around 9:00 that night the people from Davenport and Harris Funeral Home arrived to take him away. I knew I wouldn't make it through that. I had to sign some papers for them. They were very nice and extremely respectful. I didn't stay to see them take him out. That would have made it too real for me. I finally began to cry and ran into my old room. Wendy and Octavia followed me. I am so glad they were there with me. I don't know what I would have done if they had not been there.

Losing a parent is hard. Daddy had been here all of my life. I had not known a life without him. I had already experienced losing all my grandparents, but this was Daddy. I wasn't sure how I was going to take this. But there was a peace about it because he was so very, very depressed the last few years of his life. If he was going to be sad it is probably best that he went on to have peace. And, as I said earlier, he was happy those last few weeks.

I still miss him. Denise, it is interesting how you are part of the peace I have after losing some close family members. When both grandmothers died, I was able to move forward because I imagined them in heaven with you. I knew you missed them and they truly missed you. When I thought of Daddy dying and going to heaven, I thought he might be a little nervous. Then, as clear as day, I could see you in heaven with him. I imagine him in line with all of the other saints waiting his turn and there you come running past everyone, saying "DADDY, DADDY!!!!" He would have that big smile on his face and grab you and raise you high in the air like he used to do all of us when he came home from work every day. It was the best part of our day. He would raise us so high in the air that we could see the top of the refrigerator. It is such a happy thought—bittersweet, actually: you have been without him for so very long, but it is your turn now. I know you have made him feel welcome and are showing him all the people he knew on earth who have made it to heaven. It's now your turn to be with him. Give him a big hug for me . . . he is forever with me in my heart.

We wanted to give Daddy a grand funeral, one that would show what a wonderful person he was and talk about all the good he had done. Over the years, when I thought about Daddy's homegoing service, I thought I would say some words that I wanted folks to know about our daddy. Before he died, I started thinking about them. One day I kept thinking about them and I fell asleep that

A sweet picture of you with Daddy. I think it is the only
one I can find of you together. He was always behind
the camera. Photo from the Chris McNair Archives.

night thinking about what I would say. When I woke up I remembered everything that came to mind while I slept and I said to myself, "that is a eulogy." I had
never given a eulogy before, but when I woke up and put those thoughts on paper I could not imagine anyone else doing that but me. I asked Daddy if it would
be ok and he said yes, and Kim was okay with it too. So that was it. Lots of family
and friends tried to talk me out of it. They didn't think I would be able to do it.
But I felt that God had given me the words to say, and I had already cleared it with
Daddy. I promised him and I had to keep my promise.

Here is the part of the eulogy that I feel is the real essence of who Daddy really was:

Daddy taught us how to look at each person as an individual. He never said the typical things you hear folks say in private. You know, the stuff we say when we are home and nobody is there but your family. Stuff like, "you know all Black folks do this or you know all white folks do that." He would always say "well, you know, human beings do this and human beings do that." At first, I thought that was weird but later I grew to understand that he was saying that HUMAN BEINGS are good and HUMAN BEINGS can be bad. There is no race or color that is all good or all bad. Like it says in the Bible, Romans 3:23: "for all have sinned and fall short of the glory of God."

That was how Daddy saw folks. That is what made him such a wonderful communicator with folks of all walks of life. Look around this room at all the people; there are all race and creeds here with one common denominator: you all loved daddy, and you all love Mamma, Kim and me. (*I ask everyone to shake hands or hug their neighbor.*) Love has no color. Neither does death. Dr. King said it so eloquently in the eulogy at Denise, Addie Mae, and Cynthia's funeral. I was not alive when Denise died but I have had the opportunity to hear and read it for myself. It was amazing. If you ever get a chance to read the whole eulogy, you should. It was beautifully written. He said of death, "Death comes to every individual. There is an amazing democracy about death. It is not aristocracy for some of the people, but a democracy for all of the people. Kings die and beggars die; rich men and poor men die; old people die and young people die. Death comes to the innocent and it comes to the guilty. Death is irreducible common denominator of all men." That is so very true. This was one of the many amazing lines in that short eulogy that really helps you to put this in perspective. All of us are born and all of us must die. It's the part in the middle that we need to work hard on to make sure you get it right.

That was Daddy. He worked hard to love and get along with all people. He will always be remembered for that and I will take those and all the lessons he taught me out into the world to make it be a better place.

Give Daddy another hug and kiss for me. I will see y'all again one day and it will be a great celebration.

Until then, love you,
Lisa

Comfortable in My Own Skin

Dear Denise,

It's about time I wrapped up these letters, since I think I have told you much of what I would say if you were here. My quest has been to live and love in this world, particularly in the United States, as a free, Black woman. Martin Luther King Jr. wanted Black and white people in this country to coexist in peace as friends. The fruition of his dream, however, was something neither Black nor white folks knew how to embrace. The transition to the new South and the merging of the lifestyles and cultures of our two races have been far more complicated than anyone could have predicted or imagined.

I am a direct byproduct of Dr. King's dream. I have already pointed out that I am a part of the first generation of African Americans who have been able to move freely around this country, and that's an important point that I don't hear talked about much. It may not be where it needs to be today, but we sure have it a lot better than you did in 1963.

I have family and friends around your age who lived through your death and the deaths of other girls. They remember the bombings and the terror, and that shaped their perspective of life in America. They remember the "Colored Only" water fountains and being told they couldn't do things or go certain places. They were denied the right to vote by being forced to take dumb tests that no one could pass when they tried to register to vote. That's what makes me different—because I don't have those memories. You are the sister I never knew, but I also never knew some of the ways Black folks were treated when you were a girl. It makes my perspective very different. I appreciate and respect what you went through, but life was quite different for me.

I had white children with whom I went to school who were my dear friends. I spent the night at their house, and they came over to mine. This surprised, shocked, and even terrified some people, including my relatives. I told you that Dear Dear warned me not to date or bring a white boy home. One Thanksgiving after she passed away, I did invite a white guy from Dawson Baptist who was in my Sunday school class. He didn't have anywhere to go and I asked him if he wanted to come over to my house and share the holiday with us, and he accepted.

Our cousin Mamma Helen, who you know, was in the kitchen when I was cooking something, and she said, "Lord have mercy, Aunt Clara must be rolling over in her grave to know you brought a white boy home." But that is the way things are now. If we fellowship together outside of work and school, we are bound to spend time in each other's homes. We are finally seeing one another as fellow "human beings," just like Daddy used to say.

I will close here, dear sister. Oh, for the chance to talk with you and hug your neck. Maybe you would have been a bit miffed at me too since I had so many white friends. I don't know. I hope that you would understand that I was born into a different world than the one in which you grew up, and it was tough for me to fit in. At the same time, I didn't lose my life for being Black like you did. I had to learn how to be Black in a mostly white world. I hope you would be proud of me today and I want you to understand my journey, as much as I can understand it myself!

I have finally made peace with the Black side of me, and the white side of me. That is who I am, a human being, good and bad, Black and white. I have even made a joke of it. I dated a Black guy once who gave the "white girl" side of me a name: Becky. Well, I told my friend Audra about that and she said that I also have a real Black side of me, and she named my Black side LaQuesha. I love it. It is a way to identify both sides of my personality, Becky and LaQuesha. Because who among us is not a combination of all of our different life experiences? I don't bristle at being called "white girl" anymore like I used to. I have learned to laugh at it.

I love who I am now. I feel so confident with all kinds of people because my varied life experiences have been great and have allowed me to meet and interact with a wide variety of people of all races and walks of life. I am also quite sensitive to others and what they go through, especially if they are isolated or being discriminated against. I have grown from someone who was tormented and didn't like myself to someone who loves herself. I only have two regrets: One is that I wish I could have gained this wisdom in my twenties, and two, that I was thirty-five pounds lighter! LOL!! But everything is done in God's timing and in his ways. Things can only get more positive from here.

Mamma isn't well. She is very old now and in poor health. We have all moved back in the house with Mamma now: me, Kim, and her husband, Jimmie. I work for myself now, traveling the country speaking to businesses, groups, and organizations about your murder and how we can reconcile our differences. I still do professional photography, carrying on Daddy's tradition. I formed my own photography business called Posh Photographers. Daddy used to hate that I named it that. He thought I should have used my name because people knew me in the community. I understood how he felt but I really liked this name and I stuck with it.

I still hope to get married; I would like to share this wonderful life I have with the right man. I try not to think too much about it. I am definitely at peace about it and no longer sad or depressed. It will come in God's time. And I don't care what race he is as long as he loves God and is good to me. I have always said that I don't know what man God has planned for me, but if he picks him then he could be from anywhere in the world because he knows everyone and knows who is just right for me, and that's a good thing.

It's cool that I get invited to speak to people because I am your sister, and that helps keep your memory alive and knowledge of that terrible incident in the memory of others. I hope they never forget so that we will never repeat that act of hatred and violence again. I always speak with pride that Denise McNair was my

Here I am giving a speech in the 16th Street Baptist Church. I travel the country almost full-time these days, speaking to colleges, schools, businesses, churches, and corporations, sharing your story and our family's loss and talking about how we can come together as human beings. Photograph by Audra Gray.

big sister, the sister I never knew. I look forward to our reunion, which will also be an introduction, in heaven with our Lord. Until then, I will keep on working out what it means to be me and to be comfortable in my own skin. Thanks for letting me share with you.

I love you,
Your little sister, Lisa

So Long for Now

Dear Denise,

You now know more about me than anyone in the universe, other than our Lord. You know things I have not shared with another living soul. I wanted to share with you all about my life, the life you would have known and been a part of if you had not been taken away from this earth so soon. I hope I shared with you a little bit of what society has been like since you passed away.

Learning about your death is my oldest memory. Many young Black kids learned early on that they were Black, and that meant white folks hated them for no reason other than the color of their skin. That meant they would have a place of "less than" when compared to their white counterparts. That was difficult to wrap my head around, but it was compounded for me because I knew that being Black meant you could be murdered just for being Black too. That has haunted me and has stayed with me to this day; how could it not? I always wondered why there was such discrimination. It made no sense to me. I often thought that if only white folks knew me and my family and how nice we were, they couldn't hate us. I still feel that way today. Not just me and my family, but all Black families in this country.

Over the years, I learned that hatred for Black people was not in the hearts and minds of all white people. That was a big relief, but as I'm writing this, some of those ugly, hateful actions by white people that we thought were gone have reared their ugly heads again. We thought we had made progress, but it turned out that the racism in some people's hearts had not been erased, it only went into hibernation and became dormant. When the opportunity presented itself, that thinking came back to life, as evidenced when our first Black president, Barack Obama, came into office.

Your death set my life on a certain course and trajectory. Daddy said that we have lived parallel lives with you, and I have found that to be so true. I don't do much that doesn't involve you and the circumstances that are a direct result of your death. Mamma and Daddy—mostly Daddy—were often called upon to talk about you and the bombing for years. After Spike's documentary, they were asked to speak about the effects that the bombing had on them and our family. That documentary introduced the tragedy of your death to a whole new group of people who had either forgotten or never knew about it.

In the last several decades, the study of what happened during the Civil Rights Movement has been a more widely accepted interest in our country. Across the country, a number of African American museums have opened up. Many of the Civil Rights legends, icons, and foot soldiers have been sought out for interviews and speaking engagements, and many even had documentaries and movies made about them. Increased interest has arisen about the church bombing and the Civil Rights Movement in the Birmingham area. Sadly, many of those Civil Rights heroes and sheroes are passing away.

We now have the Birmingham Civil Rights Institute, which is a wonderful museum and learning institution that focuses on and chronicles the entire movement. It sits right in front of 16th Street Baptist Church on the Sixth Avenue side of the church. They also have archived stories from local activists, icons and foot soldiers. In 2013, we loaned some of your personal effects to the institute, including your toys, clothes, and shoes, and other items. There is even a piece of concrete that was embedded in your head on the day you were killed. Mamma talked about it in the documentary *4 Little Girls*. She was worried about whether the undertakers would be able to make you look normal for viewing in the casket because of the damage that concrete did to your beautiful face. The folks at Davenport and Harris said they would do their best. Mamma said they did a good job and you looked nice. I have seen pictures of you in your casket, and you did look nice. The funeral home folks sent that concrete home in a box after your death, along with other personal items you had with you on that terrible day. They gave it to our grandmother Dear Dear, who many years later took it out and shared it with the family, and then gave the box to Mamma.

Today, tour groups drive or fly into Birmingham to learn about the Civil Rights Movement. In fact, they travel all over the South, and it has become a big business for the tourism industry. Many of these groups want Civil Rights activists and martyrs' family members to speak with them. Daddy was often asked to speak, but now that he can no longer tell your story it has fallen on me to carry the torch. Kim doesn't really like speaking in public, so she has asked that I handle all those requests. I enjoy this responsibility because I love to meet new people. It allows me to keep your sacrifice and memory alive and to share my views on race, Civil

Rights, and how we must remember our history and learn to get along. It is imperative that we all—Black and white—live, love, and work together in harmony, and learn to relate to one another as human beings.

I have learned more about Dr. King in recent years and found that he left behind deep wisdom for all of us. One thing he said was, "It is no longer a choice my friends, between violence and nonviolence. It is either nonviolence or nonexistence." I find that quote to be profound, not so much in its reference to physical violence, but as it pertains to the violence of our words and what we say to and about each other. That violence also can bring about death. Our words and rhetoric reveal and fan the flames of hate and anger, which can and often does lead to physical violence. We must always stay cognizant of that.

I feel now and have always felt that if we spend time getting to know each other, we will learn to like each other, embrace our differences, and discover that we are more alike than different. At least, I have found that to be true in my own experience. Because my life has been so multicultural, I have learned that we, Black and white folks, share many things in life. All of us want love, all of us suffer loss, we have stress and anger, problems and heartaches. We work in our yards, share recipes, go shopping, love to travel and have many other things in common. At the end of the day, we are all human beings and are only on this planet for a short time.

That time is too short a time to hate and be mean to one another. Since your death so many of the relatives I loved have gone to join you: both sets of grandparents, Auntie Nee Nee, Mamma's sister; Mamma Helen, Mamma's closest first cousin; Lynn, your closest friend and our first cousin; many of our grandmother Dear Dear's relatives; Daddy's brother Uncle James, who I think was your favorite uncle; and of course now Daddy. Just as this book was about to go into production, we lost Mamma too.

This is a profound loss for me. Mamma was always my best friend. We used to talk on the phone every day, several times a day. We shared everything. She made me her confidante years ago when I was a little girl. I know things about her life that I probably should not have known but she felt comfortable sharing them with me and I always wanted to be there for her in any way I could. But sadly the Alzheimer's brought an end to that everyday conversation. I always used to say that I never wanted my Mamma to die. I even prayed that the rapture would come and we would all be taken up to heaven so that she would not have to die and I would not lose her. I thought I would not be able to function once she was gone, but so far I am still standing. As I write this, it has been less than a month—so I could still be very much in shock and in denial. Also, I remember something the well-known minister T. D. Jakes said about his mother, who also had Alzheimer's disease: he said it was the long goodbye. I believe that because I have grieved over Mamma for years. Every step of her decline took a little piece of her away from me. Many a day I have been driving and thinking about losing her or a certain part of her and I would scream, or cry my heart out. I am sure if other drivers saw me they wondered what was wrong. I have cried for her so very many times that now I find it odd that I don't seem to be crying enough. People say I will have my moments that will come unexpectedly.

I will never forget her. I will carry her with me always. I am who I am so much because of her, her love, and all she taught me. What I love so much and has been very healing for me since her death is how she loved others. We have heard from so many of her students who have credited Mamma with helping them to become the people they are today. Who would have thought a third-grade teacher could leave such an impact? Those stories have really warmed our hearts. We even had some of her former students speak about how she blessed them at her funeral. For me this means she has not really left us, because she lives on in so very many people. That is a life well lived. I know she is watching over me all the time. There is no better advocate for me with Jesus than Mamma. You hug her tight until I get to heaven and can do so myself.

I miss them deeply, but I find peace knowing that you all are in heaven together and I will be there one day. I had them for most of my life; now it is your turn to share in their love and treasure trove of memories.

Dr. King spoke about death at your funeral. Of course, I was not there but in recent years I discovered that it was recorded, and I have heard it played in the church. It is quite moving. Every time I hear it, I cry. I envision Mamma, Daddy, Dear Dear, Granddaddy Mac, Grandmother Lillie Bell, Auntie Nee Nee, and other family members and friends sitting there listening with such grief and sorrow. It is such a well-done eulogy. Although the event was very sad, his words are somehow comforting. He shared a written copy of the eulogy with our parents. There are two paragraphs that Dr. King didn't read on that day. We don't know why he didn't read them, but in the second paragraph he wrote something that has stayed with me. I have already shared with you that in my eulogy for Daddy, I quoted some of what he wrote regarding death coming for everyone.

For me, that says it all. We are all the same, we are all going to experience death, ours and that of our loved ones. We are all only here for a time and then we are gone. We don't have time to hate each other, but only have time to love one another, share with one another, enjoy each other's company, learn as much as we can about this wonderful world God gave us, make peace, and learn how to live in harmony as God would want us to. That's what we are supposed to be doing as humans in this world. All those should be our main goals so we can live in peace. I hope people will remember that, think of your death and how sad and horrible the hate that caused it was, and vow to do that no more.

Until we meet in heaven, I love you dearly and think about you every day.

I love you to heaven and back again, my sister,

Lisa

Denise
McNair, 11

Carole
Robertson, 14

Addie Mae
Collins, 14

Cynthia Morris
Wesley, 14

The 4 Little Girls Memorial Fund

The 4 Little Girls Memorial Fund, established in 1983 as a 501(c)3 private foundation by AmSouth Bank (now Regions Bank) and *The Birmingham News*, provides college scholarships in memory of the four young girls killed in the heinous bombing of the 16th Street Baptist Church on September 15, 1963: Addie Mae Collins, Denise McNair, Carole Robertson, and Cynthia Morris Wesley.

The 4 Little Girls Memorial Fund strives to honor and preserve the memory of the young lives that were extinguished in an instant by the infamous bombing of the church. Growing out of that tragedy, the 4 Little Girls Memorial Fund has awarded more than $250,000 in scholarships.

Please make a tax-deductible donation to:
4 Little Girls Memorial Fund
c/o Regions Bank Endowments and Foundations
1900 5th Avenue North, 26th Floor
Birmingham, AL 35203
Attention: Jennifer Foster, VP
Jennifer.Foster@regions.com

The Morgan Project

The Morgan Project: Teaching Civil Rights and social justice through Birmingham's history of conflict and courage.

On September 16, 1963, the day after the death of four girls in the horrific bombing of the 16th Street Baptist Church in Birmingham, attorney Charles Morgan Jr. delivered a powerful speech to fellow members of the Young Men's Business Club. Morgan condemned all present for letting years of racism and abuse go unpunished, saying they were just as guilty for the girls' deaths as those who actually planted the bomb. For these brave words, he and his family received death threats and were forced to leave Birmingham. The Morgan Project's "Conflict and Courage" lesson plan is based on the events of September 15–16, 1963, and on *A Time to Speak*, the book Morgan wrote based on the speech. The Morgan Project seeks to teach students about Birmingham's role in the Civil Rights Movement, and so inspire them to take their own stands in the face of racism and unfairness.

For more information on the Morgan Project and to make a tax-deductible donation, go to: www.morganproject.org.

Sojourn into the Past

For more than twenty years and through over ninety study trips to the American Deep South and Washington, DC, the Sojourn Project has been immersing middle and high school students from diverse backgrounds in academic, transformative, weeklong moving-classroom journeys along the path and through the lens of the modern Civil Rights Movement and America's struggles for liberty.

Through living history and learning about sacrifices made and lives taken to achieve the right to vote and equality, the Sojourn Project's greatest hope is for young people to recognize that they too can stand up to injustice and do extraordinary things. A California-based nonprofit, Sojourn into the Past has been honored by the United States Congress as the longest-running social justice education and outreach program of its kind.

For more information: www.sojournproject.org.

Index

favorite childhood, 26, 50, 67, 124–26, *125*; and trials of Denise's murderers, 41–42, 91–92, 100–104; and "white culture," 2–5, 32, 33–34, 35, 36–37, 42, 43–44, 47–49, 50–54, 55, 56–57, 60–62, 66–69, 130, 136–45, 158, 160–65, 166, 168–75, 182–83; White House visit, 154–55, *155*

McNair, Maxine (Thelma Maxine Pippen; "Mamma"), 4, 6–8, 10–12, 14, *15*, *16*, 22, *23*, 24–26, 30–31, 36–37, 39–41, *48*, 53, 55–56, 59, 62, 68, 75, 77–78, 80, 84, 86, 104, 106, 107, 114, 125, 127, 129–30, 136, *146*, 148, 163, 168, *177*, 181, 183, 188–89; "birds and bees" information, given to daughters, 51, 127, 130–31; and birth of Lisa, *6*, 7, 21, *23*, 85; and birth of Kim, 7, 10; childhood of, 25–27, 141, 150; churchgoing, 45, 46–49, *48*, 51, 114, 115–18; death of, 5, 188–89; and death of Chris McNair (her husband; Lisa's father), 178–79; and death of Denise, 4, 7–8, *15*, *16*, 15–18, 39; 45, 53, 62, 79, 84, 85, 92–93, 95–96, 107, 136–37, 139, *146*, 157, 186–87, 189; as debutante, 70, 71; and debutante ball, Lisa's participation in, 71, *73*, 74, 75; as disciplinarian, 34, 37, 43, 72, 75, 77, 91, 136–38, 141, 142; and documentary (*4 Little Girls*), 17–18, 92–99, 151, 186–87; dressing daughters, 30–31, 32, 40, 126; and family business (photography studio), 88–89, 105, 151–53, 159; health issues, 14, 27, 107, 109, 153, 156, 162, 178, 183, 189; and Jack and Jill, 71; and Lisa's debutante experience, 72, 73, 74; and Lisa's education, 36–37, 40, 51, 56–57, 77, 78, 80, 86, 141–42; membership at Lutheran churches, 34, 45, 46, 48–49, *48*, 52, 117, 118, 121, 123, 141, 162; music, favorite, 52; name of, 25; personality of, 10–11, 96; sorority, 59; as teacher, 29–32, 34, 36, 37, 51, 68, 71–72,

136–37, 139, 189; television, favorite, 26; 50; and trials of Denise's murderers, 41, 92, 100, 102, 103, 104; White House visit, 154–55, *155*

Midfield, city of, 41, 148

Midfield High School, 56–64, *58*, 74, 77, 83; Mary Jordan (classmate), 60–61, 62, 64; Theo Lawson (schoolmate), 59; Sonya (classmate), 57, *58*

Miles College, 76

Mission Impossible (TV show), 67, 124–25

Morgan, Charles, 172, 192; *A Time to Speak*, 172, 192

Morgan Project, the, 171–72, 192

Morris, Fate, 101

Morris, Greg, 67, 124–25, *125*

Mujumdar, Anil, 178

national anthem, 163

National Park Service, 45

Native Americans, 40, 171

Nealy, Jamie, *11*

Nee Nee, Auntie, 18, 74, 115, 118, 126, 127, 143, 144, 188–89

New Hope Baptist Church, 118

New York City, 166

Northrup, Cynthia, 157

Northrup, Yolanda, 157

Nunn, Barbara, 157

Nunn, Rhonda, 157

Obama, Barack, 153, 154–56, *155*, 186

Octavia (friend), 83, 178, 179

Oval Office, 155, *155*

The Partridge Family, 126

Peavey, June, 101

Pettagrue, Rev. Samuel, 118–20

Pippen, Clara Marshall. *See* Dear Dear (maternal grandmother; Clara Marshall Pippen)

Pippen, Maxell. *See* Mac, Granddaddy (maternal grandfather)